GOTTFRIED VON STRASSBURG

by

MICHAEL S. BATTS

The story of Tristan and Isolde is well known among English-speaking nations in a variety of versions, from childhood stories, the works of such great poets as Tennyson and Swinburne, perhaps through the opera by Wagner. The source of much of the English tradition is of course the *Morte d'Arthur* of Sir Thomas Malory, but this has been supplemented by the German tradition which derives in the main from the work of one man, from Gottfried von Strassburg, an early thirteenth-century poet, who gave to the then unpolished and uncourtly fable a poetic form unsurpassed by any writer in succeeding centuries.

In spite of the great interest in German studies in England and North America there has as yet been no volume devoted to a study of this author and the single masterpiece which he produced. An attempt has therefore been made to introduce Gottfried's Tristan, without technicalities and learned polemics, to English readers who may know no German (certainly no medieval German), to students and teachers of literature and to all those anxious to know something of one of the great masterpieces of world literature.

Gottfried's material is not "original," that is to say he did not invent the legend; he only remolded and interpreted it. It did not cease to develop but continued on the contrary to be reinterpreted and renewed at every period in European literature. This is the case with all myths and they cannot be studied at a single given point in time. Gottfried's work must therefore be put in perspective by reference to what preceded it

TWAYNE'S WORLD AUTHORS SERIES (TWAS)

The purpose of TWAS is to survey the major writers —novelists, dramatists, historians, poets, philosophers, and critics—of the nations of the world. Among the national literatures covered are those of Australia, Canada, China, Eastern Europe, France, Germany, Greece, Italy, Japan, Latin America, New Zealand, Poland, Russia, Scandinavia, Spain, and the African nations, as well as Hebrew, Yiddish, and Latin Classical literature. This survey is complemented by Twayne's United States Authors Series and English Authors Series.

The intent of each volume in these series is to present a critical-analytical study of the works of the writer; to include biographical and historical material that may be necessary for understanding, appreciation, and critical appraisal of the writer; and to present all material in clear, concise English—but not to vitiate the scholarly content of the work by doing so.

Gottfried von Strassburg

By MICHAEL S. BATTS
University of British Columbia

Twayne Publishers, Inc.   ::   New York

"... so will ich diesem schönsten aller
Träume ... ein Denkmal setzen. ..."

(Wagner)

and what followed it. For this reason the analysis of his poem is prefaced by a brief discussion of the development of the legend up to his time and followed by a resume of the major German literary treatments and scholarly interpretations of his work into our own time. Even in this unsettled age the myth still compels our attention, whether we see it in medieval or modern form, and it will surely continue to do so as long as we have the ability to be moved and poets to move us.

ABOUT THE AUTHOR

Michael S. Batts was born in England in 1929. He received a B.A. from King's College, London University, and a Ph.D. from Freiburg University. He taught at the universities of Mainz, Basel, Wurzburg, California at Berkeley and British Columbia where he has been head of the Department of German since 1968.

Professor Batts' major interests are classical Middle High German Literature (chiefly epic) and relations with other European literatures; comparative motif studies and numerology. He has published articles on major works of early thirteenth century literature and on problems of numerical symbolism and form.

GOTTFRIED VON STRASSBURG

Preface

A STUDY of an author in a series such as the one in which this work appears normally involves a consideration of the circumstances of the author's life, his development as a poet, the chronology of his works and so forth. None of this is possible with Gottfried von Strassburg, for we know almost nothing of the circumstances of his life, and his literary *oeuvre* consists of a single poem which, while of considerable length (nearly 20,000 lines), is nevertheless far from complete. Why, then, is this work so important?

When the concept of courtly love developed in Western Europe during the twelfth century, it found expression in a flood of literary works both lyrical and narrative. In succeeding centuries, countless variations have been made on this theme, which has remained not only a dominant subject in literature but also a potent force in the social order.[1] Yet no single story in all this time has represented the idea of courtly—later romantic —love more succinctly, powerfully, or beautifully than that of Tristan and Isolde, specifically in the version created by Gottfried von Strassburg. His work is one of the greatest achievements of late medieval German literature and stands as the epitome of the theme of love beside Wolfram von Eschenbach's version of the grail legend, *Parzival,* which portrays the noblest aspirations of chivalry.

Unlike his contemporary Wolfram, Gottfried's personality cannot be grasped through his work any better than he can be identified historically; and this is perhaps not without significance. Gottfried's self-effacement certainly in no way indicates a feeling of insecurity vis-à-vis his theme or his expression of it. On the contrary, he is clearly a very self-conscious artist. Rather, he withdraws behind the fable which had long existed but to which he has succeeded in giving its definitive form. His version crowns a development which had begun centuries before him and which remained, in the centuries following, largely in his debt.

Since the story of Tristan and Isolde is of such great significance in the whole of Western European literature, space will be given, at the beginning of this study, to a consideration of the legend before Gottfried's time, in order to allow the reader to appreciate what he made of it. Following a step-by-step analysis of Gottfried's poem, a survey will be made of its modern German versions, in order to indicate something of the perpetual modernity of the story and its meaning for our time. In so doing reference will necessarily be made to versions in other European languages and to the vast body of *Tristan* and Gottfried scholarship as well as to the general problems of Arthurian literature, with which the Tristan story was later associated. In order not to burden the reader, who may know the story only in translation or in one or the other of the numerous contemporary versions, all quotations are in English and technicalities have been avoided as far as possible. Discussion or criticism of the frequently conflicting views of past and present scholars has also been kept to an absolute minimum, but our debt to scholarship in the various areas will be apparent to those familiar with these fields and from the bibliography. We hope in this way to have produced a volume which may encourage both those interested in Gottfried's *Tristan* and those interested in the Tristan theme in general to pursue further this "most beautiful of all dreams."

Our thanks are due to the Committee on Research for a grant toward expenses incurred in the preparation of the manuscript; to the Humanities Division of the Library of the University of British Columbia for assistance in obtaining certain rare works; and to Dr. Rosemary Picozzi and Miss Beryl Morphet for reading proofs.

MICHAEL S. BATTS

University of British Columbia

Contents

Contents

Chronology

(all dates approximate)

Estoire mid 12th century

Thomas 1160–70

Eilhart von Oberg 1185–90

Béroul (I) 1190

Gottfried von Strassburg 1210–15

Tristrams Saga 1226

French prose version 1230

Ulrich von Türheim 1230–35

Czech translation (I) 1250

Heinrich von Freiberg 1290

Sir Tristrem end 13th century

CHAPTER 1

Gottfried von Strassburg—
The Poet and His Time

I Literary Allusions to Gottfried

THAT there exist no records which provide information about
the life of Gottfried von Strassburg is largely due to the
fact that he was not of noble birth. Consequently, it is not possible to trace his family history. Presumably he was a member of
the new class of burghers that was growing in the rapidly expanding cities. The only references which are made to Gottfried
are contained in the works of other poets, and in using these
caution is needed, for he is not named by any of his contem-
poraries. Only poets living some time after his death mention
him by name.

Nevertheless, the most important reference to Gottfried is
made by a contemporary, Wolfram von Eschenbach, which enables us to assign an approximate date to the composition of
the *Tristan* poem. Although neither poet actually names the
other, Gottfried and Wolfram seem to have carried on a kind
of literary feud.[1] There are numerous passages in the works of
both authors which suggest that the one is referring to and
criticizing the other by deliberately introducing similar characters
or similar situations but employing them in a manner which offers
a contrasting viewpoint. The question of priority—that is to say,
whose work is the earlier and whose the later—is exceedingly difficult to decide, for it has become apparent through recent research
that the works of both authors were not issued when completed,
but must have been circulated, as it were, in fascicles as they
were composed. Therefore, the possibility exists that each author
could later have added episodes referring to those portions of
the other poet's work which had reached him during the composition of his own poem. There is, however, at least one clear

case where Gottfried attacks Wolfram and Wolfram answers his attack; this allows us to establish a relative chronology.

In his literary excursus beginning at line 4621,[2] Gottfried vents his scorn on those whom he calls "inventors of wild tales, hired hunters after stories, who cheat with chains and dupe dull minds, who turn rubbish into gold for children and from magic boxes pour pearls of dust" (4665–72; p. 105). This is obviously a criticism of Wolfram's style and method of narration, and Wolfram duly replies to it in his *Willehalm*.[3] "What I wrote about Parzival in following carefully the story, many a man praised this. There were others also who scorned it and considered their own work better" (4, 20–24). From this we must assume a relative chronology: *Parzival* (basis for Gottfried's criticism), *Tristan*, *Willehalm*. Since we are able to assign an approximate date to *Parzival* on the basis of internal evidence—the seventh book must have been completed shortly after 1203 and the whole work was presumably completed around 1210—and since we also know that the unfinished *Willehalm* was begun after 1212, we can assume that the composition of *Tristan* falls around the year 1210.

The literary feud between Gottfried and Wolfram is of extreme importance for an understanding of the literary-historical situation, but this is not the time or place to consider it. Our first concern is to establish an accurate date for the composition of *Tristan*; in this respect the references made to Gottfried in other, later works are of no value. Gottfried's work was widely known and highly esteemed, and it is not surprising that later poets, in particular those indebted to him in the matter of style, should refer to him in laudatory and, for our purposes, informative terms. Of these poets the more important are those who attempted to complete Gottfried's unfinished work. His poem breaks off at line 19,554, and subsequently two separate attempts were made to provide a conclusion as far as possible in his style but with contemporary taste in mind.

The first of these continuators, Ulrich von Türheim, is a typical example of the literary taste of the generation after the great period which produced both *Tristan* and *Parzival*. He made the attempt to complete not only Gottfried's *Tristan* but also Wolfram's *Willehalm*, and it has been suggested that the *Cligés* attributed to him is nothing more than an attempt to complete a *Cligés* poem begun by Konrad Fleck.[4] His continuation of *Tristan* was composed at the request of Konrad von Winterstetten in the years 1230–35 and contains 3,728 lines or somewhat less than the length which, it is assumed, Gottfried had planned.[5] For our knowledge of Gottfried the only lines worthy of mention are contained in the opening passage, in which Ulrich laments the death of the original author:

We have suffered a great loss, and to the great detriment of this story, which has been left uncared for, now that master Gottfried who began this book is dead. . . . Alas, what great sorrow that death interrupted his living days unfortunately before his time, so that he did not complete this book. Since it has now come to pass that death has taken him off, I have undertaken. . . . (15–21)

The tense of the phrases "have suffered" and "has been left" seems to suggest that Gottfried had died recently. Furthermore the phrase "before his time" could be taken to indicate that Gottfried died young before he was able to complete his work. Ehrismann presumably makes this inference when he writes: "His continuators . . . lament . . . his premature death."[6] The indications are, however, too vague and, particularly, the use of the perfect tense is far too common—it is here combined with the simple past and is probably due in part to metrical requirements—for this passage safely to be interpreted as more than regret for Gottfried's death before completion of the work, that is, "before his time."

Much the same kind of thing is said by the second continuator of the *Tristan* poem, Heinrich von Freiberg, whose continuation contains 6,890 lines and whose introduction is correspondingly lengthier.[7] Much of it stems, however, from his predecessor Ulrich, and the only further information is provided by the addition of the words "von Strassburg" to the name "meister Gotfrit." Heinrich presumably composed the continuation for "her Reimunt von Liuhtenburk" in the last two decades of the thirteenth century, and there is thus no possibility at all that he could have had personal knowledge of the author of the original work.

In neither of these continuations is there any suggestion of a particular reason for Gottfried's inability to complete the poem, other, that is, than his death. The lack of any such evidence, combined with theories about the meaning of the work, have given rise in recent years to a number of suggestions as to why, or even whether, the work is incomplete. More or less the whole gamut of possibilities has been proposed. Mergell and Heimerle[8] claim that the work is finished, Knorr and Schwietering[9] that the poet was unable to bring himself to finish it, Hartsen[10] that it was symbolically left unfinished, and Weber[11] that he dared not finish it. None of these theories is based upon any positive evidence, but solely upon the scholar's own interpretation. The only concrete evidence for the length of the poem, namely the acrostic, suggests that the poem is unfinished.[12] More cannot be said.

The other thirteenth-century poets who mention Gottfried are Rudolf von Ems and Konrad von Würzburg. Rudolf, who died in 1254, was strongly influenced by Gottfried in his earlier works and pays him a great tribute in a lengthy passage in his *Alexander*,[13] some of which is worth quoting at this juncture:

This did the wise Gottfried of Strassburg do, who never in falsehood took a false step in his speech. How beautifully formed is his work! What a masterpiece is his *Tristan!* Whoever has read that knows well that he was a treasure of sweet words and a gateway of wise intent (3153–62).

Konrad von Würzburg died in 1287 and was, without doubt, Gottfried's greatest pupil and a past master in the art of style. On several occasions—in his *Herzmaere,* in the *Trojanischer Krieg* and in the *Goldene Schmiede*[14]—he eulogizes Gottfried, but his compliments, though admirably phrased, are couched in more general terms.

II *Works Attributed to Gottfried*

On every occasion on which Gottfried is mentioned, the epithet "meister" is employed, and the words "von Strassburg" are usually appended. This is the name and title ascribed to him also in the famous Heidelberg manuscript of minnesong, commonly known as the Manesse manuscript.[15] In this, the largest and most beautifully made collection of songs of the minnesingers, completed in the early years of the fourteenth century, there is a full page picture of "meister Gotfrit von

Strazburc" and a collection of his poems. The picture, which is presumably by the artist who did most of the illustrations of the collection, portrays Gottfried in typically stylized form. He is reading, or has read, to an audience of five men—although, curiously enough, the text he is holding would seem to be written on wax tablets. The depiction of such a large group of figures is unusual in the work of this artist, and perhaps it is this fact which has given rise to the suggestion that these five figures, two standing on the poet's left and three sitting on his right— the poet himself is seated—represent the five major writers referred to by Gottfried in his literary excursus. At all events, they clearly express their delight at what they have heard.[16]

The poems attributed to Gottfried in this manuscript are: a love poem (6 stanzas), a hymn in praise of the Virgin Mary (63 stanzas), and a poem in praise of poverty (12 stanzas). Although the love poem also appears under Gottfried's name (with only 5 stanzas) in the smaller Heidelberg manuscript, and although the poem to the Virgin is found in abbreviated form under his name in the Weingarten and Karlsruhe manuscripts, neither of these poems, nor the poem on poverty, is believed to have been composed by Gottfried. The love poem is quite contrary to his style, and the poem on poverty is equally unlikely to have issued from his pen, from the point of view of both style and content. The hymn to the Virgin was for a long time considered to be his work, but it is now known to be the work of a poet imitating his style. On the basis of literary allusions—for example to Hugo von Langenstein's *Martina* (completed in 1293)—it cannot have been written before the very end of the thirteenth century.[17]

However, a very different poem on the subject of "brittle fortune," which appears nowhere under Gottfried's name, is mentioned by Rudolf von Ems as having been written by Gottfried. The reference in Rudolf's *Alexander* reads as follows: "The wise master Gottfried sang that glassy fortune's strength is brittle and weak and breaks into tiny pieces when it is shining its best" (20,621–25). This poem is in all probability the one attributed in the Manesse manuscript to Ulrich von Lichtenstein (stanza 308 of his work), and on the basis of Rudolf's evidence and a comparison of the style of Gottfried and Ulrich, it is now generally accepted as the work of Gottfried. In addition, the poem immediately preceding "Brittle Fortune" in the manuscript

—"Mine and Thine"—since it is in exactly the same form and style, is also accepted as the work of Gottfried. Despite Rudolf's evidence, we are not convinced that these poems can be ascribed to Gottfried, and they are too short to allow a firm decision on the basis of stylistic criteria. The poems are, in any case, of little interest and are therefore included, at this point, in literal translation without further comment.

Fortune goes astonishingly up and down;
One finds it much more easily than one can retain it.
It wavers when one does not take good care of it.
Whom it will burden, to him it gives too soon
And from him also takes too soon what it gave;
It makes foolish him to whom it has entrusted too much.
Joy brings sorrow.
Before we are without trouble in body and mind,
Rather one finds brittle fortune.
It has fragile strength.
Whenever it sparkles before our eyes and shines its best,
Then it breaks most easily into little pieces.

People and countries could well be happy
But for two little words: mine and thine.
These brew many wonders in the world.
How they go about making men everywhere wise and mad
And drive the world around like a ball.
I believe there will never be an end to their war.
Accursed greed
Has been growing and spreading ever since Eve's time
And it leads astray all hearts and all kingdoms.
Neither hand nor tongue
Desires nor loves anything but falseness and fickleness.
Teaching and judgment are openly false.

Mention must finally be made of one other occurrence of Gottfried's name—in this case in his own work. The initial letters of the eleven introductory quatrains of *Tristan,* together with line forty-five, make up the acrostic:

G D I E T E R I C H T I

The G may stand for Gottfried's own name and the T and I are the first letters of the names Tristan and Isolde. The remaining letters of these names appear at regular intervals throughout the work and enable us also to estimate that the poem was planned to have approximately 25,000 lines. The letters occur

in a special pattern: the letters of Tristan's name embrace Isolde's
name: T I I T,   R S S R and so forth.[18] The use of acrostics is
a familiar feature of medieval works,[19] and a simple comparison
is provided by the *Alexander*. Rudolf is known to have been influenced by Gottfried, and the existence of an evident acrostic
in *Alexander* supports the assumption of a similar pattern in
Tristan. The *Alexander* poem is also introduced by a number of
quatrains of which the first letters make up the author's name:
Rudolf. The initial letters of the individual books of the poem
produce the name of the hero Alexander.

The name Dieterich is in all probability that of Gottfried's
patron, but the identification of such a common name is, of
course, out of the question. The letter G had sometimes been
thought to stand for the title Graf (Count),[20] since the remaining letters of Gottfried's name did not apparently follow. In
fact, some further letters do occur and are to be found immediately preceding the letters of the names of the hero and
the heroine. The manuscript tradition is somewhat confused in
the placing of these ornamented initial letters, but not as confused
as Ranke's edition suggests.[21] Preceding the second letter of
Tristan and Isolde—R S S R—there is an O at line 1751, which
is the second letter of Gotefrit. There is no justification for the
capitalization by Ranke of the D four lines later (1755). After
the letters T—preceding I O O I—and E—preceding S L L S—
only the Heidelberg manuscript treats the four lines as a quatrain and gives the following line a capital, but even then not a
large one. This was presumably done on the pattern of the other
letters, where each occurred twice, the second letter always four
lines later, but it is interesting to note that most manuscripts
only indicate each letter once, for example: R (1751) is found
in several manuscripts, S (1755) in none; S (1865) occurs in
several manuscripts, and R (1869) in only one. In short, it is
highly improbable that the letters D, A, and S which, in Ranke's
edition, follow O, T, and E—and which have probably obscured
the understanding of the acrostic—have any significance. The
entire pattern is as follows:

```
G                    O      T      E      (FRIT)
     DIETERICH
               T  T  R  R  I    I S   S   (TAN)
               II    SS    OO    LL       (DE?)
```

The full name of the poet would possibly have been GOTEFRIT, although this form has one letter more than TRISTAN. The name ISOLDE would have one letter less still, and it has been suggested that the oblique form ISOLDEN would have been used. In addition, it is possible that Gottfried would have named himself fully at the end of his poem if he had completed it, since it was customary for a poet to give his name either at the beginning or the end of his work. Hartmann, for example, names himself at the beginning of *Der arme Heinrich* and *Iwein* and at the end of *Gregorius*.[22]

III *The Poet through His Work*

Our only other source of information about Gottfried is the work itself, and here the difference between Gottfried and his rival Wolfram is very marked. Whereas Wolfram not only makes comments on the characters and actions in his work but also speaks of identifiable historical events and places and even of his own personal experiences, Gottfried only rarely breaks out of his anonymity as narrator, and then only in order to theorize or preach. The one exception to this rule is a statement concerning his experience of love, which will be discussed later. In viewing Gottfried's poetic creation as a source of information about its author we are, therefore, restricted to drawing rather impersonal conclusions, but these are nevertheless of considerable significance.

In the first place, it must be noted that Gottfried's source is French and that the manner in which he handles it indicates a thorough familiarity with that language. He makes none of the errors in translation which can be traced in the works of other poets. He is also versed in Latin and has studied the classical authors known and accepted in his day. In addition he has studied the rules of rhetoric. His knowledge of theological writings must have been considerable, and he makes free use of symbols and associations taken from the religious sphere. Apart from these scholastic accomplishments, Gottfried refers with evident knowledge and interest to such diverse fields as music and chess, hunting and hawking. In sum, it would appear that he was thoroughly educated in the liberal arts, as he himself prescribes for the hero of his poem.

Gottfried's concern with the details of the education of his main characters is patently more than mere embellishment or lip-service to a not uncommon literary practice, namely that of describing the upbringing of the hero in order to demonstrate his exemplary qualities.[23] Tristan's education is described in great detail, as is also his instruction of the princess Isolde. Whilst not denying the relevance of the fact that this upbringing serves to draw Tristan and Isolde closer together and to make them more suited to one another, we cannot overlook that in the education of his hero and his heroine Gottfried is portraying a form of upbringing which, to him, is an ideal without which the fullest understanding and enjoyment of life is not possible. So marked indeed is Gottfried's interest in the education of Tristan and Isolde that it has been suggested that he was possibly connected with a teaching establishment in Strassburg, which is by no means unlikely, but not convincingly demonstrable.[24]

The education which Gottfried himself had enjoyed, and his evident belief in the importance of intellectual training, contrast strongly with the attitude of his contemporary Wolfram, and nowhere does this emerge more clearly than in the lengthy excursuses with which he interrupts his narrative from time to time. These sermons do not normally give us much information about Gottfried's person, but they are significant in the interpretation of the poem and will be discussed later. The lengthiest excursus is, however, quite unrelated to the action and provides us with an interesting insight both into Gottfried's knowledge of German literary history and into his attitude toward contemporary society.

At the point where the hero Tristan is to be knighted and where one would normally expect a lengthy and colorful description of this ceremony with all the attendant details so popular at the time, we are provided, instead, with a short history of the literature of the past fifty years. The eulogization of one's predecessors in the art of poetry, particularly with a view to stressing one's own shortcomings, was a familiar enough feature of literature of the time. Rudolf's and Konrad's opinions of Gottfried quoted above are good examples. On this particular occasion, however, Gottfried places his literary survey rather differently and makes it much more extensive than usual. It is obvious that he is well aware of the present state of literature and is fully conversant with the manner in which it has developed. In his survey, he divides literature into lyric and epic and lists the individual poets and their qualities much as one would now find them in a modern history of literature, the one exception being Bligger von Steinach, whose work has been almost entirely lost to us. He is also deeply concerned with esthetic canons and takes the opportunity to criticize Wolfram very sharply—though not by name.

Perhaps there is also in this whole passage an indication of Gottfried's critical attitude not only toward Wolfram as a poet but toward the knightly class he represents. This is suggested by the very fact that Gottfried puts the literary survey in the place of what should have been a description of the most important event in the life of a knight, namely the bestowing of the accolade. In place of this description Gottfried bestows—and withholds!—his own accolade as an artist. It is reasonable to regard this as evidence of Gottfried's consciousness of his position as an artist and his position in literary tradition. He is perhaps the first fully self-conscious artist in German literature and the first example, therefore, of the artist in conflict with the prevailing spirit, or better, the prevailing social order of his time.[25]

CHAPTER 2

The Development of the Tristan Legend

WHEN Gottfried introduces the question of the source of the material for his poem (ll. 131ff.), he begins by stating that there have already been several versions of the story of Tristan and Isolde, but that these have been inadequate: "I am well aware that there have been many who have told the tale of Tristan; yet there have not been many who have read his tale aright" (131–34; p. 43). The fact that Gottfried places this statement in one of the quatrains, the initial letters of which make up the acrostic, is already a sign of the importance that he ascribes to this question, and he even repeats his statement a few lines further on, before citing what he claims to be the only true source: "When I said that they did not tell the tale aright, this was, I claim, the case. They did not write according to the authentic version as told by Thomas of Britain, who was a master-romancer and had read the lives of all those princes in books of the Britons and made them known to us" (146–54; p. 43). Only when he had read Thomas' version was Gottfried sure that he had found the right one, and he then searched diligently for confirmation of the story: "Thus I made many researches until I had read in a book all that he says happened in the story" (163–66; p. 43).

It could be that Gottfried was merely employing the familiar topos of having searched out the best available source for his story, but even if this were so and he had in fact done no research into the history of the material, it is nevertheless significant that he felt it necessary to make this claim. His claim is in fact evidence of an essential difference between the modern and medieval concepts of fiction. It is virtually impossible to speak of fiction in the modern sense in connection with the literature of this period, for, whereas one now demands of a writer that he

21

invent and elaborate upon characters and actions, it was then expected that the poet narrate the true course of events in the past, no matter how often they had previously been told.[1]

It is difficult to assess the extent to which poets genuinely believed in the truth—in the sense of factual nature—of their stories or to what extent the audience accepted them as true; but at least up to the time of Gottfried it was expected of every poet that he bring evidence of the veracity of his story by citing acceptable sources. In some cases we know that poets were actually guilty of citing spurious sources in order to lend color to their asseverations of veracity, and there may be something of this behind Gottfried's attack on Wolfram for being one of those "inventors of wild tales, hired hunters after stories" (4665–66; p. 105). Not infrequently, the characters were connected with well-known historical personages in order to give further credence to the story; and it is remarkable in this connection that as the story of Tristan was expanded from its original Celtic form to the lengthy French prose romance of the thirteenth century, his parentage and descent were made more and more complete until finally he was portrayed as a direct descendant of Joseph of Arimathea.

As a result of this attitude toward the craft of fiction, almost all the major literary works of the late medieval period are translations or adaptations, in one form or another, of already existing and familiar works. This is true for all literatures; and for German literature of the period in question French works provided the main source of material. It must not, on the other hand, be assumed that because each work is a translation, it is for this reason necessarily lacking in independence of thought and, therefore, artistically inferior. On the contrary, the poet saw it as his task to adapt the material to his time and his society, to represent truth as it appeared to him and his time. This procedure is in essence no different today when writers attempt to re-create, for example, the myths of classical antiquity in a modern setting.

Many scholarly studies have been devoted to a comparison of individual works with their sources, something which can be valuable, but which can easily degenerate into vapid generalization about national and racial characteristics.[2] The value of the comparison of a small number of fairly closely related texts lies in the extent to which it aids us in the understanding of the qualities of the individual authors and in the insight which it gives us into the development of the climate of thought in Europe as a whole. Given, then, that Gottfried had more than one possible source from which to choose, and given that we have some knowledge of these sources, we are better able to appreciate his work if we can understand why he chose Thomas and rejected the others. But first we must briefly summarize the supposed stages of development from the time of the historical Tristan to the middle of the twelfth century.[3]

I *The Preliterary Development*

The son of Talorc, King of the Picts at the end of the eighth century, was named Drust; and the names Drostan and Talorcan appear in Welsh literature (Trystan and Tallwch). A King Mark of Cornwall is attested for the sixth century by a ninth-century work, the *Vita Sancti Pauli Aureliani*. There are no historical events known to us on which the legends around Tristan could have been based; and indeed there is no reason to assume that any events similar to those depicted actually occurred. His reputation was presumably such as to justify the association with him of certain stock legends and situations—something that often happened with famous figures of the so-called Dark Ages. The central episode, in this case, is the love affair between Tristan and the wife of his liege lord; the chief supporting episodes are the slaying of the giant, Morold, and the lone journey to the mysterious woman gifted with magic healing powers, the only person capable of healing Tristan's wound. Both these latter motifs are not uncommon—the most famous example of a fight with a giant being probably David and Goliath, whereas the lone voyage (Irish: *imram*) is a motif which is more specifically Celtic; there are a considerable number of such stories, one of the most famous being the voyage of St. Brendan.[4] These stories, however, are not germane to the development of the Tristan fable, which depends upon the relationship between Tristan, Isolde, and Mark.

From a comparison of the basic action of this story with similar tales and with other versions of the Tristan material extant in Celtic literature, it is assumed that it was originally Isolde who played the active role and who attempted to seduce

Tristan from his loyalty to his lord, her husband. Although Tristan remains, at heart, loyal to Mark, he flees with her to the forest. This motif, too, is a specifically Celtic one and forms the basis for numerous works.[5] There they are finally discovered; Tristan is dying and with his last strength kills Isolde.

This tale was later radically changed by the introduction of a love potion shared—though unintentionally—by Tristan and Isolde, since by this means their love became at once mutual and excusable. They were no longer morally responsible for their actions. Even after this change the story still ended with the flight to the forest and their death, but other elements would presumably also have already been included. In particular, Morold had probably already been related to Isolde in order to provide the not unfamiliar literary situation of a woman falling in love with one whom she should more logically detest.

In these earlier stages the tale ended in what one might term an heroic manner; that is to say, Tristan was the central figure and he died heroically, in physical combat with Mark, and taking with him into death the woman that he, in the one case, did, and in the other case, did not, love. The further development of the story provides a completely new element through the addition of a second part, which does not merely have the effect of delaying the end but of completely changing its nature. To allow for this extension of the tale, the lovers leave the forest, Isolde returning to Mark and Tristan going into exile. In exile, while still in love with Isolde of Ireland, Tristan meets a second Isolde, Isolde of Brittany or Isolde Whitehand. He marries her but continues to love and secretly meet the first Isolde. His death is brought about by a poisoned wound similar to that which he had received in the battle with Morold. Isolde, who arrives too late to save him, dies of grief at his side. Through this prolongation of the story, the quality and permanence of their love is strengthened, but the ending is no longer heroic and is brought about by a means totally extraneous to the Tristan-Mark-Isolde relationship. The poet who made this change was probably also responsible for prefacing the whole work with a description of Tristan's parentage, in particular of the tragic circumstances of his birth.

Such, in brief, is the outline of what is generally accepted as the genesis of the Tristan story in the form in which it must have been known in early or mid-twelfth century. However, it must not be assumed that the stages of development represent distinct and individual works: They represent only the major changes which were introduced and which made the growth of the legend from a short tale to an extensive epic possible. The source is clearly a Celtic tale which passed not directly into England but southward through Wales into Cornwall and from Cornwall into Brittany, and back again into England. Evidence of this is found particularly in the names and the geographical location of the events. At every stage in the development, motifs from local tradition or from literary sources were introduced, so that the whole became an agglomeration of the most varied elements. If the basic ingredients of the flight to the woods and the lone voyage are Celtic, then the fight with the giant, the search for the unknown maiden with the golden hair, the slaying of the dragon, the ambiguous oath, the marriage with the maiden of the same name as the unattainable beloved, and the motif of the black and the white sails provide evidence of additions from the common stock of fairy tales and from Arabian and classical sources. At exactly what stage these elements were introduced is, of course, impossible to deduce. In fact, any attempt to reconstruct the detailed plot content of the preliterary versions beyond the immediate source of the extant works is bound to be an exercise in scholarly ingenuity. The most we can say is that the outline of the plot after its development from the early short Celtic source to the lengthy epic upon which our literary versions are based was roughly as follows:

(A) The love of Tristan's parents; the death of his mother in childbirth.

(B) 1. Tristan's early life: he kills Morold and is cured of the poisoned wound by Isolde who has sworn vengeance on the murderer of Morold.

2. Tristan woos Isolde on behalf of his uncle, is discovered as the slayer of Morold but able to save himself and complete his task through having killed the dragon.

3. Tristan and Isolde drink the love potion before Isolde's marriage to Mark. After the marriage they conceal their love from Mark for some time but finally flee to the forest.

(C) Isolde returns to Mark while Tristan goes into exile. He marries the second Isolde. Wounded by a poisoned spear, he

sends for Isolde with instructions that a white sail should
be hoisted if she is coming, a black sail if not. On the false
report of a black sail he dies and Isolde dies at his side.

This supposed source of the extant versions is usually referred
to in scholarship as the *estoire,* and its existence, at least in the
form suggested by Ranke, is disputed, for it has proved impossible to determine even the approximate place and date of
its composition. Estimates in particular of the date of composition
vary by a generation or more. On the other hand, the claim has
been advanced that no such third stage existed, but that all
extant versions derive from the earlier, second stage of development.[6] These problems need not concern us, since our interest
is in what the known authors have made of their material,
and also because it is generally agreed that some such source
as the above must have preceded them. Individual episodes are
bound to vary, since there existed, side by side with the main
body of the story, short, episodic works about Tristan, and these
could be taken up into the main work at varying points, or they
could continue to exist independently alongside the latter. A
well-known example of one of these shorter episodic works is the
Lai de chèvrefeuille by Marie de France.[7]

II   *Literary Versions before Gottfried*

It has been stated that the *estoire* or something similar is the
source of all the extant literary works and that Gottfried derived
his material from one particular version to the exclusion of others.
The question thus arises: What versions did he reject and why?
In German, the only other known version of the Tristan story
before the time of Gottfried is that composed by Eilhart von
Oberge, a ministerial from the neighborhood of Hildesheim in
Thuringia.[8] It is evident that Eilhart did not receive the impetus
for composing this work from his native Thuringia but from the
Lower Rhine area where he had settled. Here the literary climate
was much more favorable to the composition of secular works;
and it is in the dialect of this area that Eilhart writes. Unfortunately, we possess little of his poem in anything like its original
form. In all, the fragments of the work which date from the late
twelfth century contain a few hundred lines. There are also
some manuscripts of a later reworked version. In addition there
exists a Czech translation[9] of the *Tristan* poem which was made

between 1250 and 1350 and which uses Eilhart to a great extent, in addition to Gottfried and the continuation by Heinrich von Freiberg. There is also a fifteenth-century chapbook—the earliest known edition was printed in 1484—which is based on Eilhart.[10] From a comparison of these later works with what we have of Eilhart it is possible to establish that they are reasonably accurate translations and thus may represent Eilhart's version where the original is lacking.

The broad outline of the story in Eilhart's version is identical with that given above, but the history of Tristan's parents is given in a very abbreviated form. The love between his parents is open, not secret; Blancheflor dies in childbirth on the journey back to her husband's country; Tristan's father does not predecease the birth of his son. There are also several variations in the individual episodes; but the main distinction lies in the motivation of the second part of the story, and this matter will be discussed below. The plot of the second part, that is, the marriage with the second Isolde and the events leading up to the death of Tristan and Isolde, is the familiar one.

The only other version—excepting, of course, Thomas—which Gottfried could possibly have known is the French version by Béroul.[11] This work is, in part, quite similar to Eilhart but also raises some very difficult problems. In the first place, as with Eilhart, we do not have the complete work but only some lengthy fragments. Theories as to the date of composition vary widely. It has been suggested that it was written as early as 1150, but the safest assumption lies in assigning a date not later than 1190. The whole of the first part, describing Tristan's parentage and his early life, is lost, and the manuscript does not begin until after the marriage of Mark and Isolde. From this point, the plot appears as outlined in the *estoire*, that is to say, the flight of the lovers to the forest and their later return. After their return, however, the story changes abruptly. Earlier minor differences could have been easily explained as the influence of the minor episodic poems, but the latter part of Béroul's work seems to make use of an unknown tradition. While some familiar material such as the ambiguous oath is used—this too in a rather different form—other passages such as Tristan's revenge on those who have betrayed him are entirely new. So different in fact is this latter part from the earlier portions, and indeed from what we know of the legend in general, that it has frequently been suggested that a second author took up the work after Béroul had left it unfinished. This theory is nowadays discounted, but the discrepancies remain and are still a mystery. Unfortunately, the manuscript breaks off before the beginning of the story of the second Isolde, so that we are unable to assess the degree of difference fully.

If we now turn to Gottfried's main source, the first thing that we must admit is that our knowledge of it is just as uncertain as our knowledge of the other works discussed.[12] We possess only parts of the poem in its original form, and unfortunately these are from that portion of the work which Gottfried did not complete. The manuscript begins at the point where Tristan considers marriage to the second Isolde, and there is an overlapping of only a few lines. Fortunately, however, a Norwegian translation is available. This work was done by a Brother Robert at the request of King Haakon of Norway in 1226.[13] We have part of this work in a fifteenth-century manuscript, and the complete work in a seventeenth-century manuscript which appears to have been accurately copied from the original. From a comparison of the translation with those portions of Thomas' work which are available, we can judge that the translation has been done with a fair degree of accuracy, but that the translator has deliberately reduced the length of the work, largely by omitting details of description and of emotional states, without abbreviating the action in any way.

The narration of events leading up to Tristan's birth, for example, is detailed, but the episode of the love potion is passed over with a brief reference: "After Tristan had taken the glass and drunk half the contents he gave the other half to Isolde, and they were both deceived by the drink they had drunk, for the servant had taken them the wrong one. It gave them both a torment and anxious days all their life, an insatiable hunger and yearning for each other. Tristan was moved to love Isolde and Isolde Tristan with such great force that they could do nothing against it" (p. 157). This passage requires 475 lines in Gottfried's poem! Otherwise, the plot follows the outline of the *estoire* with one major distinction concerning the motivation of the second part, which will be discussed in the following paragraphs.

In addition to this Norwegian translation, there exists a Middle

English poem known as *Sir Tristrem* which, though radically abbreviated, nevertheless clearly and probably directly, derives from Thomas.[14] This work serves as additional corroboration of the accuracy of the Norwegian.

Having outlined what we know of the three literary versions of the Tristan legend which preceded Gottfried's work and which he either knew or could have known, we must ask ourselves: What are the differences between these versions? What influenced Gottfried to accept Thomas and reject the others? To what extent has Gottfried, in his turn, altered his source?

There is clearly a much closer relationship between Eilhart and Béroul, in both material and style, than there is between these two and Thomas. The distinctions between the versions can be exemplified through a simple comparison of two basic elements of the plot: the flight to the woods and the efficacy of the potion. In Eilhart and Béroul, the lovers are caught more or less *in flagrante* and are condemned to death, but they succeed in escaping. Their flight is thus literally a flight, an escape. Their life in the woods is by no means an idyllic existence, and something of the older tradition here shows through in the description of the harshness of the conditions under which they live. When the King discovers them sleeping with the sword between them, he magnanimously does not take them while asleep but withdraws. When they awaken, they flee further into the forest.

The return of the lovers to the court is motivated by the fact that the efficacy of the potion is limited in time—in Eilhart to four and in Béroul to three years. At the end of this period, they go to a hermit and confess their regret, whereupon the return of Isolde to Mark is arranged. Tristan, whom Mark cannot forgive, is forced to go into exile. There is no logical reason why Tristan should not, at this juncture, meet and marry the second Isolde, since he is no longer under the influence of the love potion. He is, nevertheless, still in love with the first Isolde, and this is explained by the poet as—to put it simply—force of habit. The latter part of the story then follows the traditional pattern.

The version by Thomas offers a completely different scheme. In the first place, the flight to the woods is not an escape from a perilous situation, since the lovers have not been discovered. The King, unable to bear the uncertainty of his suspicions,

banishes them from court. In effect, he renounces his claim to
Isolde. The lovers withdraw to the forest, where they lead an
idyllic life, self-sufficient to each other. When the King finds
them sleeping with the sword between them, he is able to
persuade himself that his suspicions were unfounded and thus
call them back to court. Only at a later date are they caught
in flagrante, and only at this point is Tristan in any danger. He
now flees into exile, but, since the love potion is not limited in
time, his love for Isolde remains as strong as ever. The non-
consummation of the marriage to the second Isolde and the
clandestine visits to his true love are thus adequately motivated.

All other variations between the three versions are insignificant
in comparison with these basic differences, and they are so basic
that it is difficult to accept the theory of a single common
source for all three versions. We feel that the question of the
priority of the two viewpoints regarding the efficacy of the love
potion cannot be answered satisfactorily, but that in all probability the limitation to a specific time is a later development. We
suggest, however, that by the middle of the twelfth century
two distinct versions existed, in one of which the effect of the
potion was limited, in the other not. It is unlikely that the
extant works derive directly from the same single version known
as the *estoire.*

More important than these problems is the question of
Gottfried's choice of Thomas for his source rather than Eilhart
or Béroul. All three versions precede Gottfried by a generation
or more—though the relative chronology is quite uncertain—but
it is clear that Thomas was much closer in spirit to Gottfried's
time than was either of the others. Again, our comparison can be
restricted to the motivation of the flight to the woods and the
use of the potion.

In Eilhart's version, Tristan and Isolde are found out through
a trap set by the King and the dwarf. They are tried like felons
and condemned to death by burning. When Tristan succeeds in
escaping on the way to execution, the King is furious and
demands that Isolde be put to death immediately. He is anxious
to make her death as unpleasant as possible and therefore agrees
to the suggestion of a leprous knight that she be turned over to
him and his fellow lepers to be treated at their will—a fate "ten
thousand times worse" than death at the stake.[15] The party taking

Isolde away encounters Tristan after his escape, and he is able to free her. On their flight to the forest, they meet a hermit who exhorts them to renounce their sinful love, which, of course, they cannot do. When the love potion loses its effect, however, their first thought is to return to this hermit and confess their sin.

In the behavior of Mark toward Tristan and Isolde, in his harshness and his cruelty, the traditions of a much earlier and less courtly generation are reflected. The lovers are treated as common criminals: Tristan is not accorded the privileges of his rank, nor Isolde the respect and restraint due her sex. Such an attitude was unacceptable to Gottfried and his time, and he would, therefore, naturally turn to Thomas, whose version avoids all such violent scenes.

More significant, however, is the treatment of the love potion and the motivation of the love between Tristan and Isolde. In Eilhart and Béroul, the potion is somehow more closely related to black magic: love is viewed as an uncontrollable, unwelcome, and even evil force. Eilhart apostrophizes the potion and, on occasion, feels obliged to excuse Tristan's behavior—which he is unable to condone—by reference to the compulsion of the potion. The same attitude underlies the introduction of a representative of the church, who exhorts them to renounce their sinful behavior, a representative to whom they resort as soon as their minds are freed from the evil influence of the potion. This view of love derives from an earlier period when literature, or rather, the class in which this literature developed, had not freed itself from the restraint laid upon it by the church, when courtly love had not yet developed into that all-powerful and positive force which found such intense expression in, for example, minnesong. To Eilhart, the potion is the only thing that excuses the love of Tristan and Isolde, whereas Gottfried's generation needed no such excuse and rejected any association of religion with love, in the sense that love could only be comprehended within the religious framework. In this respect, Thomas offered a far more acceptable version, in that the potion is not limited in time and the positive values of the love relationship are stressed to the complete exclusion of all religious forms.

Gottfried was thus bound to reject the Eilhart version for a basic reason, namely because of the lack of positive commitment on the part of the author to the love relationship between Tristan and Isolde. The Eilhart version represents a much earlier and more primitive stage in the development of courtly love. Perhaps also it was composed for a less cultured level of society. That Thomas is much more modern in his portrayal, even though he is roughly contemporary with, or even earlier than, Eilhart, is evidence merely of the varying rates of regional development. Thomas was at the very center of this development, at the court with the most advanced and sophisticated culture, whereas Eilhart was on the periphery.

This is not to say that Gottfried remains entirely uninfluenced by Eilhart. His examination of his predecessor's work has undoubtedly left its traces as, for example, in his direct refutation of one aspect of his compatriot's version, namely the tale of the golden hair. Eilhart's King Mark declares that he will marry only the maiden from whose head has come the golden hair which a swallow has let fall while building its nest. Tristan, therefore, sets out in search of the unknown beauty. Gottfried, when he has adequately motivated Tristan's journey to Ireland to woo Isolde, discusses this other idea in a passage of twenty-eight lines and dismisses it as utterly absurd. He ridicules both the idea of a swallow fetching a hair so far to make its nest and the idea of setting out to search the world for the owner of a single hair. He concludes: "The king who sent his council abroad, and his envoys—had they gone on a mission in this style—would have been dolts and fools" (8625–28; p. 155). Gottfried is, in other words, concerned with the lack of *vraisemblance,* something which did not disturb earlier and less sophisticated audiences. Eilhart's style of presentation is much more in the manner of the minstrels for whom such extravagant features were meat and drink; and in rejecting such aspects Gottfried is seeking to eliminate not only the uncourtly but also the fantastic elements.

This concern for *vraisemblance* is something that distinguishes Gottfried not only from Eilhart but also from Thomas, though in a lesser and more subtle degree, for Thomas organizes his material more carefully. Gottfried can, however, be critical even of Thomas as when, for example, he rejects Thomas' statement that Mark was given some of the potion to drink on the wedding night when he asked for wine. "No," says Gottfried, "none of that potion remained; Brangane had thrown it into the sea"

(12,655–56; p. 208). Whatever the motive for this emphatic rejection of Thomas' version—Eilhart does not mention the potion at this point—it is important to note that Gottfried is capable of disagreeing also with his avowedly "genuine" source.

IV *Gottfried and Thomas*

The detailed comparison of Gottfried's work with his source is an exceedingly lengthy and laborious task which has been undertaken more than once and with varying degrees of success.[16] It is complicated by the necessity of using not the original but the Norwegian translation by Brother Robert and the Middle English *Sir Tristrem*. It cannot be our purpose here to enter into detail on this subject. The discussion of the general differences between the two versions will be based on the comparison of only two scenes, which have been chosen to illustrate, at the same time, the difference between Gottfried and Eilhart.

When suspicion is aroused against Tristan and Isolde, traps are laid for the lovers who endeavor either to avoid them or to turn them to their own advantage and confirm their innocence. The scene we are to discuss is the last in the series of plots and the content is as follows:

Eilhart	*Thomas*	*Gottfried*
The dwarf persuades the King to send Tristan on a journey, so that he will visit Isolde before leaving.	Mark, Isolde and Tristan have been bled.	Mark, Isolde and Tristan have been bled.
	Only Tristan is asked to stay with Mark and Isolde.	Mark keeps only Isolde, Tristan, Melot, Brangane, and a maid in the chamber.
The dwarf will strew flour on the floor; 100 men will wait outside; he will hide under the bed.	The lamps are extinguished. The dwarf strews flour on the floor.	The lamps are veiled. Mark leaves his bed to go to matins.
Tristan agrees to go but determines to see Isolde first.	Brangane sees the flour and warns Tristan.	Melot strews flour on the floor and departs with the King.
	Mark goes out with the dwarf.	Brangane sees the flour and warns Tristan.
Tristan sees the flour but decides to take	Tristan leaps to Isolde's bed.	Tristan sees the flour. Tristan leaps to Isolde's bed.

| the risk; he leaps over the flour; old wounds break open and bleed. The dwarf under the bed shouts and Tristan leaps back but is weak and leaves a footprint. He is taken by the armed men. | His vein opens and bleeds. He remains the night there. He leaps back. Mark finds blood in Isolde's bed; she says her hand bled. Mark sees blood in Tristan's bed. Renewed suspicion. | His vein opens and bleeds. He stays briefly and leaps back to his own bed. Mark finds blood in Isolde's bed; she says her vein bled. Mark sees blood in Tristan's bed. Renewed suspicion. |

The Eilhart version radically differs from those of Thomas and Gottfried, since this is the scene which leads to the downfall of the lovers. It is the turning point in his version. In Thomas/Gottfried the scene is merely one, the last one, in a series, and at the end the King is no more sure of their innocence nor convinced of their guilt than he was before. After this scene he, therefore, has recourse to the ordeal on the advice of his council. Generally speaking, the emphasis in Eilhart is on action and violence. The characters are crudely drawn—the dwarf is pathologically envious, the King rages, even the author (in the chapbook) curses the wicked potion—and the whole scene is very uncourtly, with the dwarf hiding under the bed and the hundred armed men lurking outside. Finally the lovers are captured, bound, and thrown into confinement.

As depicted by Thomas, the scene is much more subdued and refined, but Gottfried nevertheless finds considerable room for improvement and embellishment.[17] The basic differences are these:

Thomas

Only Tristan is to remain but later Brangane is also there.
The dwarf spreads the flour *before* the King goes out.
Brangane warns Tristan *before* the King goes.
Tristan remains with Isolde through the night.
Isolde says her hand bled.

Gottfried

The group as named remains: Mark, Isolde, Melot, Brangane, Tristan and the maidservant.
The dwarf spreads the flour *after* the King has left.
Brangane warns Tristan *after* the King goes.
Tristan stays briefly with Isolde. Isolde says her vein re-opened and just ceased to bleed.

The number of persons remaining in the chamber is of no particular significance, but it is evidence of Gottfried's more careful planning. A very noticeable error on the part of Thomas —probably not the fault of Robert—is the spreading of the flour before the King has left. This is corrected by Gottfried, who also narrates more logically that Brangane warns Tristan after the King has gone to matins. He also adds that there was just enough light for Tristan to see the flour. This has been objected to on the grounds that the lights have been deliberately dimmed, but we believe that this is an addition planned by Gottfried (in Thomas the lights are extinguished) partly in order to make the judging of the distance for the leap more credible; but it is also very relevant to Gottfried's statement that love makes the lover blind to all danger and to his reference to Tristan as "the love-blind Tristan" (15,186; p. 241). Despite his love-blindness, Tristan is able to see the danger, and the plotters do not succeed in using the darkness to deceive the lovers. This is a very Gottfriedian kind of embellishment and supports the contention that Gottfried has here expanded without being bound by anything in his source. In Thomas' version, Tristan remains the rest of the night with Isolde, but Gottfried depicts him as returning to his bed after a brief space of time and lying there deep in thought until morning, worried, presumably, by the knowledge of the telltale bloodstains. Finally, Isolde's excuse that her hand has bled is expanded, in Gottfried, to the more convincing claim that her vein has reopened and has only now ceased to bleed.

In addition to these alterations, there are several minor additions which one may assume to be the property of Gottfried and not aspects omitted by Thomas' translator. In the first place, the scene is introduced by a description of the good humor of the group after having been bled; this provides a contrast to the underlying tension and the danger for the lovers. The tension is later stressed by the fact that the King rises, dresses, and leaves for matins in silence, and while attending the service is unable to pay attention. In Thomas the King merely says that he is tired of lying in bed and will go to matins. When the King returned, says Thomas, he saw the blood in Isolde's bed and then saw that Tristan's bed was bloodstained. In Gottfried, the King first looks at the unmarked floor before going to his bed. Having found the bloodstains in his bed, he then seemingly jokes with Tristan and, in so doing, pulls the covers off him—whereupon he abruptly falls silent.

Also in the course of this scene, Gottfried uses imagery which is clearly of his devising and which was partly discussed above. Tristan, the love-blind, views the trap as a kind of trial of his strength, as a gamble with Isolde as the prize. The irony of his action lies in the Pyrrhic victory he gains, for although he succeeds in leaping across the flour, his vein breaks open and he is forced to return to his own bed. The King, too, is defeated, for he has no proof, only renewed suspicion. This expansion in Gottfried contrasts also with Eilhart who considers Tristan's situation at this juncture and says that his love compels him to do this, and that this love is against nature, being caused only by the potion: "For Tristan was a sensible man who would certainly have loved in natural and reasonable measure, but the power of the potion made him forget all wisdom" (p. 82).

These minor details, one may assume, are Gottfried's attempt not only to make the whole scene more natural and logical but also to integrate the play of emotions and tensions with the action and with the symbolic pattern of imagery. His independence in this scene is further underlined by the introductory passage of sixty lines which separates the scene from the preceding attempt to trap the lovers. In this passage, Gottfried inveighs in person against malicious envy in the guise of friendship, referring here to the machinations of Melot and Marjodo. These men, the dwarf and the chamberlain, are apostrophized as snake and cur and as snakes in the form of doves. Although Tristan and Isolde are on their guard against them, Mark is persuaded by them to make one more trial of the lovers, and the result is the ensuing scene.

Finally it must be noted that in Gottfried's poem the scene closes with a description of Mark's renewed doubt and suspicion, and this is picked up in the opening lines of the following passage as a preliminary to motivating his next move, the summoning of the council. In Thomas this was probably treated more briefly. In the Norwegian translation, Mark's feelings after this scene are indicated only in one brief sentence, but this is then followed by the passage which, in Gottfried, begins the next scene.

The other scene to be discussed has been chosen, on the one hand, because it provides an opportunity to compare

Gottfried directly with Thomas—and the latter with Robert—and
on the other because it again affords an interesting comparison
with Eilhart, though not, of course, textually. This scene, in
which the lovers are discovered in the garden, does not occur
in Eilhart's version; for there they have already been discovered
as a result of the scene just discussed. The comparison is, therefore, not a direct one; but it is a question of comparing the treatment of what might be termed the discovery scene. In Eilhart,
the betrayal depends upon the bloodstains, the telltale footprint
and, presumably, the testimony of the dwarf who had hidden
under the bed; it is thus a direct result of the plotting. In Thomas
and Gottfried, this scene has, or had, been altered to provide
only the climax of a series of *inconclusive* attempts on the part
of Mark to discover the truth. Another episode on the same
pattern had, therefore, to be introduced in order to bring about
the separation of the lovers. This is the scene in the orchard
where the lovers are found *in flagrante*. Since the Thomas version
has survived, part of the scene will be quoted in direct translation, to afford the possibility of comparing, in some measure, his
style with that of Gottfried and Robert.

Robert

But Tristan could in no way restrain his will and his desire, and
therefore he used every opportunity to obtain it, and thus it went
on until one day they both lay together in the garden and Tristan held

Thomas	Robert
Queen Isolde in his embrace and they thought themselves quite safe. By strange chance the King comes upon them, led there by the dwarf. He thought to take them in the deed but thanks be to God they were sleeping in a seemly manner. The King saw them and said to the dwarf: "Stay here a while. I will go to the palace and bring here some of my barons. They shall see how we have found them. They shall be burned when it is proved upon them."	Queen Isolde in his embrace. And when they thought they were quite safe they were nevertheless surprised by the King who came with the dwarf and the King thought he would catch them both in sinful deed. They were sleep-ing, however, and when the King saw them he said to the dwarf: "Wait for me while I go to the palace and I will bring here the highest of my people that they see in what kind of situation we have found them, and I shall have them burned at the stake if they are found together."

With this Tristan awoke, but made no sign until the King had gone into the palace. Tristan then arose and said: "Alas, Isolde, my love, awake now. We are betrayed. The King has seen what we have done and goes to the palace for his men. He will, if he can, have us taken together and sentenced to be burned to ashes. . . .

While the King spoke, Tristan awoke but made no sign. Then he stood up quickly and said: "It goes evil with us, beloved Isolde. Wake now, for plots are made against us and we are trapped. King Mark was here just now and has seen what we have done and has gone now for his people into the hall; and if he finds us together he will have us burned to ashes. Now, my beloved, I will go away but you need not fear for your life, for they can bring no firm accusation against you if no one but you is found here alone.

Gottfried

Mark went there [to the garden] at once and found his mortal pain there. He found his wife and his nephew tightly enlaced in each other's arms, her cheek against his cheek, her mouth on his mouth. All that the coverlets permitted him to see—all that emerged to view from the sheets at the upper end—their arms and their hands, their shoulders and their breasts—was so closely locked together that, had they been a piece cast in bronze or gold, it could not have been joined together more perfectly. Tristan and Isolde were sleeping peacefully after some exertion or other.

Only now when the King saw his woe so plainly, was his irrevocable affliction brought home to him. Once more he had found his way. His old overload of doubt and suspicion was gone—he no longer fancied, he knew. What he had always desired had now been given him with certainty. All his past efforts to rid himself of his doubts had now ended in living death. He went away in silence. He drew his councillors and vassals aside. He made a beginning and said that he had been told for a fact that Tristan and the Queen were together, and that they were all to accompany him and take note of the pair so that if they were found there as stated he should be given summary judgment against them in accordance with the law of the land.

Now Mark had scarce left the bedside and gone but a short way when Tristan awoke and saw him receding from the bed. "Oh," he said, "what have you done Brangane, faithful woman? God in heaven, Brangane, this sleeping will cost us our lives. Isolde, wake up, poor lady. Wake up, queen of my heart. I think we have been betrayed." "Betrayed" exclaimed Isolde! "How, Sir?" "My Lord was just standing over us. He saw us and I saw him. He is just going away and I know for a fact as sure as I shall die, that he has gone to fetch help and witnesses—he means to have us killed. Dearest lady, we must part, and in such a way that, it seems, such chances of being happy together may never come our way again." (18, 193–27; pp. 280–81)

There are, first of all, the following material changes to note. In Thomas, the King is brought there by the dwarf who remains behind when the King goes to fetch witnesses. This makes no sense, since when the King returns, the dwarf is entirely forgotten and the lovers have ignored his supposed presence. In Gottfried, the King arrives by chance, the watchers—Brangane in fact—having been taken by surprise. In the Thomas version the King's speech to the dwarf presumably awakens Tristan, but in Gottfried the King quietly withdraws and Tristan wakes only as he is already leaving. Tristan must, therefore, assume that Mark has gone for witnesses; he cannot know it, as he does in Thomas, through hearing the King speak to the dwarf. In Thomas no reference is made to what Mark tells his barons; in Gottfried, Mark tells them that he has been told that Tristan and the Queen are together and that they should accompany him as witnesses. Tristan's speech varies slightly in that Thomas' hero fears that they will be burned if caught together, whereas in Gottfried this is reduced to the fear that it will cost them their lives. Gottfried has further removed Tristan's claim that Isolde will be in no danger if found alone. The remainder of Tristan's speech (not quoted here) is similar, but in Gottfried Isolde's reply is considerably longer.

These are, however, only the more obvious differences, the material changes which Gottfried has made. Noteworthy also are his additions both before and in the course of the scene. In Thomas—that is, in Robert's version—this scene follows immediately upon the description of the return of Tristan and Isolde from the grotto. The sentence preceding the passage quoted above reads as follows: "Then he sent for them that they should come home in peace and joy, since he had abandoned his anger against them." Since, therefore, nothing is said of a passage of time, the impression is given that their discovery follows immediately on their return, and this may have been one of the considerations which prompted Gottfried to expand at this point. In his version the scene is prefaced by a lengthy excursus which begins with an analysis of Mark's situation after the return of the lovers.

Gottfried discusses Mark's love-blindness, the fact that he knew Tristan and Isolde were lovers but refused to "see" it and, therefore, lived a life without honor. He exonerates Isolde from all blame, since she behaved openly and honestly; but Mark is blamed for being blinded by sensual lust. This analysis of the strained situation leads to a discussion of the surveillance of the lovers and the morality of surveillance per se. Virtue, says Gottfried, will guard itself; nothing destroys it so much as putting a watch on it. He claims that a woman will naturally be tempted to do what has been forbidden to her and makes a startling comparison with Eve in the garden of Eden. This is followed by a consideration of the struggle, in woman, between instinct and honor and by a commendation of those who conduct themselves with moderation, that is to say who have singleness of purpose and constancy.

Gottfried concludes with a praise of womanliness and the fortune of men on whom a truly womanly woman has bestowed her favor. Only after this lengthy discussion Gottfried returns to his diatribe against surveillance and continues with a description of how *Isolde* sought to avoid it. He takes the brief reference in Thomas to *Tristan's* use of every opportunity to satisfy his desire and describes in detail *Isolde's* state of mind, *her* arrangement of the meeting with Tristan, the preparation of the bed, the sending of the messenger, the precautions against intruders, and finally, the unexpected appearance of the King. This analysis of the situation and the diatribe against surveillance are entirely lacking in Thomas and are, obviously, Gottfried's invention. The significance of this and other excursuses will be considered elsewhere; for the moment it should be noted that this one occupies no less than 392 lines and also serves to smooth over the otherwise rather abrupt transition in addition to indicating the passage of time between the return from the grotto and the discovery.

There are also numerous additions within the scene. In the first place, in Thomas we find no description of the lovers other than the statement that they were sleeping in each other's arms "in a seemly manner." Gottfried considerably expands upon this with a beautiful description of the lovers which emphasizes their inextricably close union, and he changes Thomas' reference to their sexual union to a perhaps less subtle but more humorous one.

Thomas' plain statement of fact that the King saw them is expanded by Gottfried to a further analysis of the King's state of mind. The irony of this situation lies in the King's discovery of what he claimed he wanted to know, what he in fact already *did* know, but what he can now no longer ignore. To this Gottfried adds the subtle indication of Mark's shame, for he cannot bring himself to say to his councilors that he himself has seen the lovers. He can only say that he has been "told for a fact" that Tristan and the Queen are together.

Tristan does not blame the actual discovery on Brangane—who plays no part in Thomas—although the motif of betrayal has been retained. In Thomas, the dwarf is the deliberate betrayer but is then forgotten; in Gottfried, Brangane inadvertently betrays them, but Tristan, in addressing her, does not associate her with the betrayal. On the contrary, he uses the term "faith*ful* woman," and the assumption is inevitable that discovery was their fate.

Finally it should be noted that Isolde's reply to Tristan's short speech (not quoted above) has been extended by Gottfried. In Thomas, Isolde speaks merely of the pain of parting and the future lack of joy. Though their bodies are separated, their love can never be sundered. She then gives him the ring, and they kiss on parting. Gottfried has seized the opportunity to expand, once more, on the physical and spiritual unity of the lovers. Isolde says that her life is in Tristan's hands and that he should take care that no other woman come between them. She then gives him the ring. After this action, however, she proceeds with her speech, recalling past joys and sufferings and stressing their physical interdependence. Tristan should guard his life, as she will guard hers, since they are but one flesh and blood; and if he dies, she will die too. Their kiss, says Isolde, is a seal *(insigel)* that they will remain loyal to one another until death. This is developed from Thomas where Isolde gives Tristan the ring and calls it contract and seal *(brief und sigel)* before they kiss at parting. In Thomas, this speech has approximately one hundred words, in Gottfried over three times as many.

It cannot be our task here to discuss in detail either Thomas'
interpretation or his style, for we are only concerned to see in
broad outline what kind of source Gottfried had at his disposal
and how he dealt with it. Very briefly, then, it may be said that,
although Thomas' version is a great improvement over Eilhart
insofar as greater emphasis is laid upon the psychological motivation of the characters' actions and the inner logic of the fable,
there are, nevertheless, numerous shortcomings both in the
material and in the presentation. Apart from its somewhat
matter-of-fact style, Thomas' version suffers from inconsistencies
in action, from repetitious passages, and from a general lack of
color and depth. Broadly speaking, Gottfried has treated these
and other aspects in the following manner: he has been at pains
to correct material incongruities and to establish a logical and
natural order of action. He is concerned, in other words, to
establish the *vraisemblance* of the text, although he, too, has
retained minor inconsistencies. Especially noticeable is the increased stress on psychological motivation and on the presentation of character. Here Gottfried has added a great deal, partly
through improved narration, but more significantly through
direct analysis and comment by the narrator on the thoughts and
emotions of his characters. In addition to direct analysis, frequent
use is made of symbolic association and description, which also
aids in providing the background with a degree of depth which
is lacking in the colorless style of Thomas. Finally one may
say that Gottfried has lavished great care on the formal structure
of his work by composing individual scenes and episodes with
an eye to balance and symmetry. This is particularly evident in
his introduction of balanced groups of characters and in the
organization of the ebb and flow of action within the individual
scenes.

CHAPTER 3

Gottfried's Tristan: *An Interpretation*

IN recent decades, there have been several interesting attempts at a comprehensive interpretation of Gottfried's *Tristan,* and some progress has been made even though, on the surface at least, there is little sign of any agreement.[1] After the narrowly positivistic-historical approach and the moralizing attitude of the nineteenth century have been shaken off, other impediments to an understanding of the poem remain, some inherent in the work, others in the nature of criticism and the limitations of the critic. One primary difficulty is the incompleteness of the poem, although this must not be overstressed, since it is evident that the chief burden of Gottfried's thesis has already been imparted and the actual ending is predetermined. Another difficulty is the nature of Gottfried's style, which renders the meaning of many passages elusive. So consistent in particular is—one assumes!—his use of irony that the same passage may mean quite opposite things to different readers. And there naturally is the question of the source. Since this story is known to us in other versions, it is inevitable that we have these, to some degree, in our minds and, consciously or unconsciously, judge or interpret Gottfried's work in relation to them. The poet himself openly discusses his source, thereby indicating that his audience, too, may have known something of Thomas or other versions and that he is inviting comparison. While we feel that this is improbable, it is by no means impossible.

The question of the relationship of Gottfried's work to its sources is, in itself, not a simple problem to resolve, but it raises, in addition, the more delicate issue of the possibility and desirability of interpreting this—or for that matter any—work of art as it would have been or should have been understood by the contemporary audience, whether or not this audience knows the earlier versions. This issue is far too large to be debated here, involving, as it does, not only the distinction between how the work was understood and how, or even *if*, it was intended to be understood. Nevertheless, the subject must be broached, if only superficially, in order to make our position clear. We do not believe that it is ever possible to comprehend completely the intended meaning of a literary work at a period remote from that in which it was written. This is largely due to the impossibility of adequately re-creating the contemporary intellectual climate; and one of the great weaknesses of modern criticism of this period is to approach literature with preconceived ideas about the spirit of the age, and to assume that the author was representative of any and every aspect of the age which the critic believes to have been characteristic. However, this is not to say that we should not attempt to understand these works. We should merely be aware that we are actually combining the spirit of two ages (that of the original work and our own), but this does not in any way detract from the value of the undertaking.

Our intention, then, in this chapter is to attempt a general statement of the meaning of the poem on the basis of the text alone and in the order in which the poet has set it down, with the scantest possible reference to philosophical, religious, and other movements of the time. Since it is manifestly impossible to discuss every aspect of the story in detail, the interpretation will be centered around certain episodes which are thematically, structurally, and symbolically related. The emphasis which is thereby laid on an analysis of the action is not merely unavoidable, it is also deliberate, for it is our contention that action in medieval literature means character; it *has* or *is* meaning. All too often, the author's or narrator's comments are weighed too heavily against the meaning of the action or the statements of the characters. This has been especially the case with Gottfried, whose predilection for didactic divagation has led to an overemphasis of those often platitudinous discussions which may well express Gottfried's views but which do not necessarily have any particular value for the interpretation of that aspect of the story which provided the point of departure.

I *Tristan's Early Life—the Love Potion*

To begin with some rather obvious facts, it may seem strange to a modern reader that in one of the world's great love stories the hero and heroine do not fall in love until halfway through the poem (*ca.* l. 12,500) and are permanently separated three-quarters of the way through the poem (after l. 18,358). Furthermore, the first half of the poem is devoted not to the early history of the lovers but to a description of the life of Tristan alone, preceded by the story of the life and death of his parents. The story of the hero's parentage is important in medieval literature, since character was viewed as determined by heredity, by what is known in medieval German as *art* (nature in the sense of character). For this reason, the biographical introduction is frequently met with in epics, and in the case of Gottfried's *Tristan* it is even shorter than might have been expected. The work would, if completed, have consisted of 25,000 lines or approximately the same number of lines as Wolfram's *Parzival;* and yet the story of Rivalin and Blancheflor takes up only 1500 lines, as opposed to the 4,500 lines in which the story of Parzival's parentage is narrated. In Gottfried's poem, the love story of Tristan's parents also foreshadows, to some degree, the experiences of Tristan and Isolde and must, therefore, be discussed in some detail.

Gottfried portrays Rivalin as a model knight. Although still a youth, he possesses all the virtues traditionally assigned to the perfect nobleman: beauty, loyalty, generosity, charity, and so forth. His one weakness is his strong desire for adventure and his rash and unpremeditated actions. "He overindulged in pleasures dear to his heart and did entirely as he pleased. . . . It never occurred to him to overlook a wrong . . . but he returned evil for evil, matching force with force" (262–73; p. 45). Gottfried excuses this on the grounds of his youth and emphasizes the apology by using the words *child* and *childhood* three times in rhyme within the space of eight lines. However, in his first adventure Rivalin is successful, for he defeats and subjects his overlord Morgan, thereby greatly extending his dominion. At this point, his own affairs apparently no longer hold sufficient interest for him, and he determines to seek out the very center of chivalric culture in order to improve himself and extend his reputation.

This standard motif of courtly literature—and, it should be added, of life—brings him to the court of King Mark in Cornwall.

Rivalin is well received in Cornwall, and his assiduity as a courtier makes him very popular even before the great festival at Tintagel. Gottfried describes the setting and the activities of this festival in subtle and delicate tones tinged with a considerable amount of irony and humor, so that—although the impression is partially given of a pleasure-seeking and effete society—the stage is most beautifully set for the unfolding of the love of Rivalin and Blancheflor. The whole arrangement seems to be there only to serve as a fitting backdrop to the meeting and courting of these two young people, and something of Gottfried's degree of interest may be deduced from the fact that this passage occupies almost four hundred lines, as opposed to the mere sixteen lines for the entire story of the campaign in which Rivalin is wounded.

The youthfulness and inexperience of Rivalin are made very evident by his bewilderment at Blancheflor's behavior. Only very slowly he realizes that she may be attracted to him and begins to reciprocate her feelings. She, in turn, is portrayed as, if anything, more innocent than he, for she does not at first understand her feelings at all, even attributing them to some form of magic. Only after a lengthy analysis of her own emotional state does she conclude that she is in the grip of love. She it is who then makes the first move toward provoking a mutual understanding. Neither in any way resists the power of love, nor indeed has any reason to do so. They do, however, keep their love a secret, which is in the true courtly fashion.

The first enjoyment of their love is interrupted by the short campaign in which Rivalin takes part and in which he receives what is, by all accounts, a mortal wound. We have here the first indication of what Gottfried meant when he said earlier: "His downfall was due not to malice . . . but to the tender years that accompanied him" (292–94; p. 45). His headstrong nature has obviously carried him into the thick of battle, just as later he rushes without proper preparation into the battle with Morgan.

Foreshadowing a later situation, Blancheflor comes to Rivalin disguised as a physician. Sorrow at first deprives her of strength, but she revives and her kisses put strength into Rivalin. Their love is consummated, and she conceives a child. Love is here shown as having the power to heal and revive, although Gottfried stresses—perhaps unnecessarily—that Rivalin could not have recovered had God not so desired. But death cannot be cheated, and at the very moment of their union Blancheflor conceives the child which is to be her death.

Both are, as it were, only temporarily reprieved from death through the strength of Blancheflor's love. Rivalin is still destined to die in the near future in the same manner in which he so nearly died; and Blancheflor carries with her the death she took from Rivalin. Their desire for life, after this first meeting and the consummation of their love, is strong. They are more closely united than before:

He was hers and she was his. There Blancheflor, there Rivalin! There Rivalin, there Blancheflor! There both and there true love. . . . And when they could decently arrange a meeting, their worldly joy was so complete . . . that they would not have given this life of theirs for any heavenly kingdom. (1358-72; pp. 58-59)

And yet their love is destined to pass away rapidly, as the flowers of the great May festival have faded. Again external circumstances intervene, this time compelling Rivalin to return to Parmenie. The behavior of Blancheflor and her lover when he breaks the news to her is an almost exact parallel to the earlier "deathbed" scene. It is now Blancheflor who collapses "unconscious and as if dead" (1428; p. 59), while Rivalin is so affected as himself to weaken and almost faint. She revives only when he takes her into his arms and repeatedly kisses her. Gottfried again emphasizes the mutual strength which the one derives from the physical presence of, and contact with, the other. They elope to Parmenie, but the end comes quickly. Rivalin dies in battle and Blancheflor in premature childbirth induced by her despairing grief at his death.

Although beautiful in its own way, this story of Rivalin and Blancheflor is on a different plane from that of Tristan and Isolde, for they are both unprepared for love and inexperienced in the world, like children. Neither gives a thought for the future and the inevitable problems it will bring, that is, the inevitability of trials and suffering. This is expressed most distinctly in regard to Rivalin, of whom Gottfried says: "He did as all young people do who never think ahead; he shut his eyes

to care and lived for the sake of living. . . . Just when the early
sun of his worldly joy was about to shine out dazzlingly, his
evening, hidden from him until then, fell suddenly and blotted
out his morning" (301–18; p. 46).

The same is true, though perhaps to a lesser degree, of
Blancheflor. The two have a fleeting glimpse of happiness and
grasp at it, living for the day and for each other. But their union
is not such that they can resist or withdraw from the world,
and Rivalin, therefore, departs on a campaign at the risk of
his life and later bluntly announces his intention of returning to
Parmenie, apparently without a thought for Blancheflor's position.
Their love, insecurely founded and not properly comprehended
by them, is doomed to be a transitory thing. For the fable as
related by Gottfried the significance lies more in the future, in
the fruit of this tenderly tragic relationship.

Tristan is conceived in the shadow of death, at the moment
when Blancheflor through the strength of her love has recalled
Rivalin from death. But conception is not a blessing for her;
it is death itself. The circumstances of Tristan's birth are, therefore, tragic in every way: his father is dead, his mother dies in
giving birth to him, and his country is conquered. At the moment
of his birth, even he himself is under the shadow of death, for
Morgan would surely have connived at his destruction had he
known of Tristan's existence. But, although his birth is surrounded
by tragedy, he is also in the truest sense of the word a love-child.
The purity of the love of Rivalin and Blancheflor and the
poignant circumstances of his conception predestine Tristan to
experience both love and suffering; and while Rual may choose
his name for the circumstances of his birth (*triste* = sad), it is
his parentage, his breeding, and his *art* that determine his
destiny.

The place of Tristan's parents is taken by Rual and Floraete,
whose very names relate them to Rivalin and Blancheflor; and
his early life, though passed under the latent threat of danger
from Morgan, is a happy period. His first acquaintance with
care is the discipline of study, but he soon applies himself with
such diligence, purpose, and talent that he becomes a master
in every area of accomplishment, intellectual or physical. It goes
without saying that every hero of a medieval epic is abundantly
supplied with superlative qualities, but, as we have seen above,

Gottfried has more than a passing interest in the question of education. Tristan has a natural ability to absorb all forms of learning, and his studies are carefully planned to provide him with a perfectly balanced education until he is at home in any situation and place. In addition, through travel at home and abroad, he is experienced in the ways of the world.

This upbringing stands him in good stead after his abduction by the Norwegian merchants, when he comes to Mark's court in Cornwall. He uses his accomplishments, first as a huntsman, then as a singer and a linguist, to impress the court and make himself welcome there. He gradually unfolds his talents to Mark, who enthusiastically exclaims: "You can do everything I want— hunting, languages, music. To crown it let us be companions. You be mine and I will be yours" (3722–26; pp. 91–92). Since Tristan wants nothing better than to agree, he is soon firmly established and even more the darling of the court than his father had been before him. The parallel is indicated by Gottfried's use of similar terms in reference to their popularity. Of Rivalin he had said: "Rivalin was pleased by the court, and the court was full of his praise. He was liked and esteemed by rich and poor. No stranger was ever loved more" (509–13; p. 48). Of Tristan he says: "From that time on, Tristan was a courtier much beloved among them. The King and his household kept good company with him, and he too was so obliging to rich and poor alike, that, had it been possible to have done so, he would gladly have pampered them all" (3486–94; p. 88—cf. 3748ff.).

Tristan's popularity is, nevertheless, distinctly different from that of his father. Rivalin had come to Cornwall in pursuit of knightly excellence and was, therefore, portrayed as taking part in a tourney. Tristan's introduction to the court is effected by his skill in dressing the stag and in playing and singing. In other words, his success is due primarily to his style of living; and the impression this makes on the court is important for our estimation of the standards that prevail there.

Because Rivalin betook himself to Cornwall, we must assume that Mark's court had a reputation for knighthood; and yet from Tristan's reception there we must also assume that life was un-sophisticated, almost rustic. There is a lack of style and polish that evidences itself in the rough-and-ready manner in which they are accustomed to hunt—as though this were an occupation rather than an art—and in their amazement at Tristan's singing and playing. This obviously reflects, to some degree, on the character of the King, and it is not without significance that the latter offers, in return for his company, something *he* knows about: "Fine clothes and horses I'll give you as much as you wish" (3734–35; p. 92). Curiously enough, in all this time, Tristan does not spare a thought for his homeland.

This life of pleasure is interrupted by the arrival of Rual who, though at first warmly welcomed by Tristan, brings news which is more than a little unwelcome. If, at first, Tristan is unable to express his feelings at the revelation of his true birth, because the change has come too suddenly, when he does express himself it is to show resentment at being deprived both of his real and his adopted father. Rual, whose patience has already been tried by hearing that Tristan has given himself out to be the son of a merchant, is justified in rebuking him; but his claim that Tristan still has two fathers—himself and Mark—does not alter the fact that, in reality, the relationship between him and Tristan has been reversed. Rual is no longer Tristan's father and natural protector (he had always given Tristan preferential treatment over his own children). On the contrary, Tristan is now in the position of father of his country, and Rual's appearance is thus a call to duty and responsibility to a country which Tristan has almost forgotten and to a manner of life for which he clearly has no taste.

Tristan's abduction had already manifested the difference in outlook between Rual's sons and himself, for it was they and not Tristan who wanted to go to the ship to buy hunting birds. They asked Rual to buy Tristan a bird, knowing that they would then be included. Tristan himself showed no interest in this typically knightly pursuit, preferring to play chess and demonstrate his other intellectual talents, a preference which leads to his abduction. In Cornwall his life has been that of the courtier, passing the time in the exercise of artistic and intellectual accomplishments—quite a different kind of life from that of his father, whose natural habitat had been the tourneying ground and the battlefield. Now that he knows that he is the rightful ruler of a rich country, the serious part of life begins, and Rual is not slow to suggest that Tristan now ask his uncle to knight him so that he can assume his rightful position.

When King Mark asks his nephew if this is what he wishes, Tristan replies in a remarkably evasive manner. In a lengthy speech (40 lines) he talks about how, if he were wealthy, he would love to be a knight, provided that he would not be a disgrace to chivalry; how regrettable that he has not been trained for knighthood from an early age, and how he would not have remained unknighted had he known the true facts of his birth. He concludes by saying that it is right and proper that he should now make up for this, but one could hardly say that he willingly agrees. With a reluctance that stands in marked contrast to his father's behavior Tristan goes through the ceremony of knighthood and returns to Parmenie. He is, of course, warmly welcomed by his late father's dependents and sets about the task of freeing them from Morgan, although not, it would appear, with any great enthusiasm. His attack on Morgan is unchivalrous and not properly prepared and leads to a very dangerous situation for Tristan who, after killing his enemy, loses the initial advantage and is surrounded by Morgan's followers. It is again Rual who, in his concern for Tristan, comes without previous arrangement to his assistance and saves the day. The country is liberated, and Tristan is installed in his rightful position.

Tristan now acts like his father; he decides to leave his newly gained position and return to Mark. As a reason he states that Mark has made him co-regent—an exaggeration—and heir, and that he is, therefore, compelled to go. The distress of his followers is described in very strong terms; they even go as far as to say: "It would have been far better for us if we had never seen you" (5817–18; p. 120), but this makes no impression on Tristan. His father had been unable to show interest in peaceful administration, and now Tristan is unable to find satisfaction in a situation which requires this kind of responsibility of him. He therefore leaves for Cornwall, following in his father's footsteps, but for quite different reasons. Not for him the desire to improve his reputation as a knight; his aim is largely the evasion of worldly responsibilities and restrictions.

The parallels between Tristan's early life and that of his father are much closer than a mere superficial resemblance deriving from what might be thought of as stock situations. In both cases they leave their land after successfully defeating

Morgan and handing over affairs of state to Rual, and come
to the court of Mark. During his stay in Cornwall, Rivalin fought
in a campaign on Mark's behalf and received a wound which
was pronounced mortal. Tristan now fights with Morold after
his (second) arrival in Cornwall and receives a wound that
is also apparently mortal. Rivalin was saved from death by
Blancheflor; Tristan can only be healed by Queen Isolde. The
situations are similar and in both cases lead ultimately to a
similar cure and a similar love scene; but in Tristan's case his
plight is made more difficult since the only person capable of
healing him is not his beloved but his sworn enemy, the mother
of his later love.

Tristan makes two journeys to Ireland. On the first, he goes
disguised as a minstrel and is able to obtain the healing of
his wound from the Queen after promising, in return, to
employ his gifts instructing the younger Isolde in the social
graces. After his return, his eulogy of the princess is indirectly
responsible for his second, and even more dangerous, trip;
for the machinations of those jealous of his position force the
King to reverse his decision to remain single, with Tristan as
his heir, and to select Isolde as the only possible consort and
Tristan as the only person capable of carrying out the wooing
mission. While the first journey led to Queen Isolde, the second
is to obtain the hand of her daughter; and the lives of the
two protagonists become ever more closely involved.

Tristan's slaying of the dragon in order to win Isolde and
his rebuttal of the Steward who claims to have performed the
deed is a masterpiece of descriptive and narrative technique,
full of humor and satire, but it must be passed over at this point
in favor of a consideration of the developing relationship between
Tristan and Isolde, whose lives now become strangely intertwined.
After killing the dragon, Tristan lies unconscious in the pool
until the three women—the Queen, Isolde and Brangane—accompanied by Paranis, set out to find the real hero, since they are
convinced that the Steward, who claims to have killed the dragon,
was not responsible. It is, fittingly, Isolde who first sights Tristan
and, even more fittingly, the gleam of his helmet that betrays his
presence. This must be the helmet given to him by Mark and
surmounted by Cupid's arrow, for we have earlier been told
"how Vulcan . . . devised his helmet, and in token of Love's

torment raised the Fiery Dart upon it" (4943–46; p. 109). It is she, too, who recognizes him as Tantris the minstrel.

The difficulties of all concerned are now apparently resolved, for Tristan can obtain immunity for himself and the Queen proof of the Steward's falseness, together with a champion to maintain their cause. The irony of the situation does not become apparent —not, at least, to the two Isoldes—until the discovery of Tristan's true identity. Not only has the Queen now twice restored to life the man she had sworn to destroy, but she is also in the position of having placed her honor in his hands, of being, so to speak, at his mercy. The promise of immunity is admittedly the prime motive for not avenging on Tristan the death of Morold, for the dishonor brought by murdering a guest would be greater than that of not avenging a relative; but there is the added necessity—immediately stressed by Brangane—of requiring Tristan's services. Isolde's subtle distinction between Tristan and Tantris, therefore, makes no impression at all. After Brangane enters the scene, it is her counsel that prevails, and it is she who is largely responsible for the practical decisions that are now taken. There is a personal reconciliation, followed by the inclusion of the King and the extension of the peace pact to their respective countries. The marriage of Isolde to Mark is to set the seal on this, and public announcement of the betrothal is made following the confrontation between Tristan and the Steward, in which the Steward is made the laughing stock of the court.

Before discussing the voyage to Cornwall, we must pause and consider the relationship between Tristan and Isolde at the moment of their embarkation. Both have been portrayed in the most glowing colors as they made their entrance at court, separately, it is true, but in like manner. The Queen first leads in Isolde, followed later by Brangane leading Tristan. The arrival of Tristan and Isolde is described in minute detail and in a similar pattern. First their general appearance and figure are described. This is followed by a detailed description of their clothing, including some repetition of detail. For example, on Isolde's dress, "where the clasps go, a tiny string of white pearls had been let in, into which the lovely girl had inserted her left thumb. She had brought her right hand farther down" (10,935–41; p. 185). Over the surface of Tristan's clothes "lay a net of tiny pearls, its meshes a hand's breadth apart" (11,115–17; p. 187).

Both of them wear a kind of chaplet inlaid with precious stones, in each case of four different kinds. The description concludes with a reference to their bearing. The greetings which the Queen and Isolde bestow as they enter are also paralleled by the greetings exchanged between Tristan and Brangane and Tristan's fellow countrymen. When Tristan and Isolde take their seats, they are placed symmetrically, Isolde on the right of the Queen, and Tristan on the left of the King.

This close resemblance in appearance and the extreme handsomeness and beauty of Tristan and Isolde also recall the similarity of their upbringing. Tristan had enjoyed a thorough and comprehensive education and was particularly skillful in playing, singing, and composing. Isolde, too, even before Tristan's first visit to Ireland as Tantris, had had this kind of education, but she had lacked finesse until Tantris became her tutor. She acquired every skill that he could offer as though to the manner born; and soon she was as admired by her father and the Irish court as Tristan had been by Mark and his court. In addition, Tristan had taught her how to conduct herself in the world, so that she would be well received, pleasing to both God and man.

Tristan and Isolde are thus perfectly suited to one another, and yet as they are seated, one on either side of the King and Queen, there is a rift between them that goes deeper than the superficial difference in social status. Isolde, intending to rescue Tantris, found that she had rescued her enemy. She then lost her respect for her tutor Tantris and her good will toward her potential deliverer from the Steward. No hint was given in the bath scene that her refraining from killing Tristan was due to anything but her purely feminine nature. She felt anger and hate and wished to avenge her uncle, but "her tender womanliness prevailed, and it snatched her from her purpose" (10,255–56; p. 176). She is, therefore, not only unable to take vengeance on the slayer of her uncle, but indebted to him for saving her from a fate worse than death; and this she cannot but resent.

To crown it all, Tristan is now instrumental in taking her away from her home to a distant land as the betrothed of an unknown king. At every step, as her life becomes more involved with his, her aversion is increased by circumstances, and Gottfried portrays with great psychological insight the manner in which, to express her resentment, Isolde stresses her hatred of him for the murder of her uncle, although her mother, who is more closely concerned, has been able to forgive and forget. She even claims that his saving her from the Steward was unnecessary, since, had she married him—previously she had claimed she would rather die—she could have remedied any defects in his character. Tristan's masculine logic in refuting these points is naturally not well received. Only a special stroke of fate could now bring these two together, and this is provided by the love potion.

What is this potion, and what does it represent? The potion has been brewed by the Queen, who, of course, intends it for Mark and Isolde on their wedding night, so that they will be united in love. The fact that the potion is now drunk by Tristan and Isolde is the crowning irony of fate, which reverses all previous trends. Formerly the Queen had wanted the death of Tristan, but unwittingly had twice saved his life. The potion she now entrusts to Brangane is intended to bring life and love to Mark and Isolde, but, instead, is to be the "death of both of you [Isolde and Tristan]" (12,489; p. 205).

Whereas previously everything had conspired to turn Isolde more and more away from Tristan, this trend is now reversed. The irony of this situation underlines the fortuitous but, at the same time, complete and irrevocable quality of love. It comes suddenly, overwhelmingly, and invalidates all previous arrangements; it is an elixir that unexpectedly and wholly permeates a person and changes the course of his life. That is the magic power of love, and that is the significance of the potion. Gottfried does not use it to excuse this relationship which he so strongly affirms, nor is he concerned to demonstrate the unfortunate consequences of the blind choice of love. His affirmation of love does not make the potion superfluous; it is a symbol rather than a necessary adjunct of the plot.

It is significant that this scene is enacted at sea. They are secluded in a harbor, and even aboard ship Isolde is secluded in her chamber. After the turbulence of the open sea they are in placid water, and there is a pause, a suspension, as it were, of action. The entourage has gone ashore, and the appropriate steward is not at hand to fetch wine. On such small matters does fate depend. The abruptness of the change of heart that now takes place is emphasized by its following immediately upon a conversation which Tristan concludes with the assertion that Isolde will soon be married to a king who will give her all she can desire. After they have drunk the potion, the ship sails on, but while outwardly all is still calm, there is in their hearts an inner turbulence, of which only Brangane knows.

Both Tristan and Isolde rapidly succumb to love, and in this they considerably differ from Rivalin and Blancheflor, who had at first no comprehension of the nature of their feelings. Indeed, there had been no sign that Rivalin had even noticed Blancheflor until her greeting and a veiled hint of her own feelings prompted him to turn his thoughts to her. Their struggles were, therefore, conditioned only by inexperience and unawareness, and as soon as they realized that they loved each other, there was no further hindrance to their desire. In the case of Tristan and Isolde, both immediately perceive what has happened; for the whole course of their life has made them ready for just such a moment. It is only the situation in which they find themselves that places obstacles in their way. Tristan is bound by ties of loyalty to Mark and a desire to maintain his honorable reputation; Isolde has no such ties, but is restrained by a feeling of embarrassment and shame, partly because her feelings run counter to her obligations, but largely because she has, until recently, expressed hatred for the man she now loves. Yet such is the power of this attraction that both overcome their scruples in a very short time and, recognizing in the other the familiar tokens of love, begin to make mutual advances. Driven perhaps also by the knowledge of the brief time before them, they soon confess their love, and the first steps are taken toward their union with the exchange of glances, vows, and kisses. The continual presence of Brangane makes them so sick with suppressed desire that Brangane is forced to bring the affair into the open—for fear they will otherwise die—and allow them their will.

The scene which now follows, the consummation of the love of Tristan and Isolde, is a repetition, in a different form, of the earlier scene between Rivalin and Blancheflor. Then Blancheflor had come disguised as a physician, but now Love comes to the sick Isolde as a physician, bringing with her Tristan, who is suffering from the same sickness. Both are suffering from a fatal malady, namely love; their only possible cure lies in the consummation of that love. Rivalin had been dying of a mortal wound and was saved from death through the power of love in Blancheflor, through her ability to give him life while taking death into herself. The sickness of Tristan and Isolde is of a deeper nature, and the consummation which preserves them from death also gives them strength and a unity which remains indissoluble through life and into death. Gottfried insists on the necessity of physical union. Without it, Tristan and Isolde would have perished; through it, their absolute union is sealed, and never again can they be separated; the death of one will mean the death of the other. When Brangane explains to them what has happened in regard to the love potion, and that this will assuredly mean their death, Tristan joyfully affirms acceptance of what his fate has brought him: "If my adorable Isolde were to go on being the death of me in this fashion, I would woo death everlasting" (12,499–502; p. 206).

II *From the Love Potion to the Love Grotto*

Tristan and Isolde are unable to remain on the ship, to remain, as it were, outside society. They are recalled to the world of reality. Although Tristan has abandoned loyalty toward Mark as a man and accepted his love for Isolde and the consequences thereof, it is, nevertheless, his bounden duty to bring her to Mark. Isolde, too, accepts this without question, without considering the possibility of escape. The justification for this will be discussed more fully in connection with the lovers' return from the grotto and in the discussion of Gottfried's relationship with his audience. For the moment, we must accept that Tristan's loyalty to Mark constrains him to allow the marriage to proceed, and that the marriage is the first in a series of deceits and not, in itself, more or less important for being the first. The fact that Isolde is able to devise a ruse to conceal her loss of virginity —by persuading Brangane to substitute for her on the wedding night—serves mainly to emphasize the special providence that protects lovers. It also provides evidence of the insensitive nature of Mark, who is unable to distinguish between the two women, between, as Gottfried puts it, gold and brass.[2] This is the first intimation we have of the insensitive-sensual nature of Mark, a theme which is to assume increasing importance.

The two episodes following the wedding are of lesser significance; they are typical of the standard stock of themes so popular in all forms of narrative of the period. Isolde's attempt to have Brangane murdered, in order to prevent her from telling tales, brings out, through the subsequent reconciliation, Brangane's complete devotion to her mistress. The Gandin episode, in which the Irish knight demands and receives Isolde in payment for singing—the King having rashly offered him in advance "anything of mine"—serves, on the one hand, to emphasize the weakness of the King and on the other the cleverness of Tristan. In a broader sense, it puts Tristan in a much better light than Mark and gives him a certain moral right to Isolde, whom he has now won, as it were, on his own behalf.

The first really significant episode is that in which, for the first time, the lovers' secret is discovered. The episode consists of two parts: the dream in which Marjodo sees a boar rush into the palace and, unhindered by anyone, break into the King's bedchamber, trampling on and soiling the bed; and Marjodo's action on waking. The dream foreshadows future events; but these events now get under way when Marjodo wakes and discovers his friend's absence. He follows Tristan's tracks in the snow through the moonlit orchard to Isolde's chamber. Here there is no light, for the candle is concealed by a chessboard, and Marjodo must, therefore, feel his way near enough to Isolde's bed to convince himself of their guilt. Being himself more than a little in love with her, his love now turns to hatred not only for her but also for his friend Tristan. He is not, however, sufficiently clever to disguise his feelings, and his very silence puts Tristan on his guard, who in turn warns Isolde.

The motifs and symbols of this episode are to recur in varied form throughout the remainder of the work. The dream itself clearly relates to Tristan, who has as an emblem "the image of him, whose courage is boundless—the Boar—on his escutcheon" (4941–42; p. 109), and whose courage reduces the courtiers around him to impotence. The scene enacted in the dream is not, however, to be fully exploited until very much later. In this particular scene, the dominant theme is the contrast between light and dark. Gottfried has already made extensive use of light symbols in establishing a relationship between Isolde, her mother, Brangane, and Tristan. Her mother is the dawn, she

herself the radiant sun, and Brangane the full moon. The bright-
ness of Isolde's appearance is matched only by that of Tristan
in the scenes at court in Ireland; and it is he who has always
stressed her radiance ever since he returned to Cornwall after
his first visit to Ireland:

Never again shall I believe that the sun comes from Mycene. Perfect
beauty never shone forth over Greece—here is where it dawns. . . .
Let all men . . . see how the new Sun following on its Dawn, Isolde
after Isolde, shines across from Dublin into every heart (8273–83;
p. 150).

It is not necessary to see in these and other references an
established and logical pattern, but rather an association of ideas.
In the present scene, there is a sharp contrast between light and
dark, between the moonlit orchard and the two darkened rooms,
between the snow and the dark footprints. Even the chessboard is presumably chequered, and it throws a dark shadow
from the candle. But it is not Tristan and Isolde who are the
children of darkness; it is Marjodo, the jealous friend, who must
feel his way in the dark, first to Tristan's bed and then to Isolde's.
Night is the time of love, and love is a secret thing. It is
Marjodo, the figure of darkness, who is now prepared to betray
this secret and to drag it into the light: "Hatred and anger
prompted him to be so unmannerly as to divulge their affair
and make it known then and there. But his fear of Tristan . . .
restrained him" (13,609–16; pp. 220–21). Afraid, then, of making
the secret public, he tells it only to Mark.

The pattern of light and dark, of love and hate, dominates the
following episodes, which cannot be discussed in detail. The
alternation of plot and counterplot, of suspicion of guilt and
belief in innocence, brings with it mounting tension and a gradual
involvement of other persons. It is first Marjodo, the friend
turned enemy, who acts to poison the King's mind and persuades
him to try to trap Isolde by asking such questions as whom she
would want to look after her should he be away. Brangane
comes to Isolde's aid and turns the trap to the lovers' advantage,
so that the King is convinced of her innocence. Marjodo then
turns to Melot, the dwarf, for aid, and although Melot is un-
successful in his attempt to trap Tristan with a false message,
he does discover their secret meeting place and arranges for

the King to eavesdrop on the lovers. This scene takes place at night, and again there is a marked contrast between light and dark, between the figures of Tristan and Isolde in the moonlight and the King and Melot in the darkness of the tree. The shadows cast by the eavesdroppers come between Tristan and Isolde but protect them as well; and the lovers are again enabled to turn the situation to their advantage by keeping their distance and engaging in what can only be described as double talk. They are by now so well attuned to one another that they can even deceive the King into believing in their innocence at the same time as expressing to each other their love and their sorrow at being kept apart.

It is not long, however, before Marjodo and Melot, the cur and the snake as Gottfried calls them—the one representing the dog biting the hand that fed it and the other innate evil and cunning "and the snake was more cunning than all the other animals of the field" (Gen. III, 1)—join forces and succeed in persuading Mark to make one further attempt to betray the lovers. In this episode, the scene shifts back to the bedchamber, and the action represents the fulfillment of Marjodo's dream. The pattern of light and dark, which was previously established and which was repeated in the orchard scene, now culminates in a setting which is even more expressive of the conflicting forces, since it is deliberately and painstakingly prepared. In this scene, Brangane joins Tristan and Isolde, so that the two sides are ranged three against three in deliberate confrontation.

The elaborate preparations begin with Mark having himself, Tristan, and Isolde bled. While they are recovering from this, the stage is carefully set by the plotters, and all other persons— with the exception of a maidservant who plays no role—are excluded. The chamber has been deliberately darkened, not this time by the lovers, but by the plotters; and when the King rises before daybreak to go to matins, Melot strews flour on the floor and leaves, too. The trap has now been set, and the lovers are left alone. Brangane warns Tristan of the trap, and Tristan, forewarned, finds nevertheless enough light to see the flour and is able to judge the distance to Isolde's bed. The very knowledge that a trap has been set incites him all the more and, as a boar will turn and attack blindly when goaded, he determines to leap over the flour. He succeeds but his success is also a failure. He gains only a Pyrrhic victory, for the vein where he had been bled opens, and the blood stains the King's bed.

The boar dream of Marjodo has thus come true, but the plotters have been no more successful than Tristan, for there are no prints in the flour, as there had previously been in the snow leading to Isolde's chamber. The King, on returning, is at first relieved to see the flour undisturbed, but then he finds blood both in his own and in Tristan's bed; and although this is not proof, it is a basis for suspicion. To this extent, then, the lovers have lost: whereas previously each plot had been turned to their advantage, this time the very inconclusiveness of the result provides the King's mind with reasonable grounds for suspicion, and he, therefore, casts off his fellow plotters and determines to take the matter into his own hands. This is an important turning point in the relationship between the lovers and Mark. From now on the character of their involvement changes, as Mark takes the private quarrel into the public sphere.

Having failed to achieve certainty with the aid of his private advisers, Mark turns to his political councilors for assistance, requiring proof in public of Isolde's innocence. This leads to the much discussed episode of the trial by ordeal, it, too, being a popular stock motif in literature throughout the ages, occurring in many forms and with every conceivable kind of twist.[3] In this case, we must bear in mind that it was still implicitly accepted in many quarters, although the church, in Gottfried's time, condemned its use. It is evident that Gottfried's application of the motif and his comments on the action represent a condemnation of a hypocritical practice. Be that as it may, Isolde takes the ambiguous oath to the effect that she has never lain with anyone save Mark and the pilgrim—Tristan in disguise—who fell down with her while carrying her ashore from the ship on the way to the place of ordeal. Her innocence is apparently proven.

Tristan has not been present at the ordeal, having left the scene immediately following his appearance in pilgrim's disguise; and there follows a curious episode in which he goes to great lengths to obtain a magic dog from his friend Gilan. To do this, he has to rid his friend of a troublesome giant named Urgan. Tristan is successful and after obtaining the dog, Petitcreiu, sends it to Isolde, for the bell which the dog wears around its neck has the power to banish all care from the person who hears it. At first impressed, Isolde soon breaks off the bell in order not to be happy as long as Tristan is sad. This episode thus briefly symbolizes their relationship: Tristan willingly risks his life for the love of Isolde, while she, suffering, just as he does, from their enforced separation, is unwilling to be comforted in any way, but prefers to suffer with him. Although she never lets the dog out of her sight, but cherishes it as a love token, she has no use for the bell.

On receipt of the news that Isolde's innocence has been established, Tristan returns to court and is received with all honor. And yet nothing has really been resolved. Melot and Marjodo are still watching and waiting, and Mark's position has become even worse than before. His insistence on a public demonstration of Isolde's innocence makes it impossible for him, when Tristan and Isolde are unable to conceal their feelings, to afford to overlook the signs, for the public must also be watching and seeing what he sees. His decision to allow Tristan and Isolde to leave court and go where they will is, therefore, less of a magnanimous gesture than would at first appear. He is forced to take action, and it is noteworthy that again he does so formally and publicly. The insistence on the oath has, in other words, brought Mark no further than the previous, more private attempts at reaching the truth. On the contrary, he now appears publicly to doubt the oath. He must believe his own eyes and accept the consequences of what he sees. The lovers are finally free to go where they will and do what they will. They are released from the burden of care and suffering and in the same situation as when they first enjoyed their love on board ship far away from the everyday world.

If the shipboard scene in which Tristan and Isolde drink the love potion is the structural center of the poem, there can be no doubt but that the episode of the love grotto is the climax of their relationship and of the entire work. On this episode Gottfried has lavished every art and artifice of which he was capable, and on the understanding of it depends necessarily the interpretation of the whole poem.

The grotto is truly a temple of love, dedicated to and by love in ancient, heathen times; and yet until its occupancy by Tristan and Isolde its true purpose has never been fulfilled.

Every aspect of this marvelously conceived structure is an allegory of the attributes of love. The smooth circular wall signifies the simplicity, and its whiteness the purity, of love; while the breadth of the chamber signifies the power of love and the green marble floor its ever renewable, self-renewing quality. The height of the chamber demonstrates to us the loftiness of love's aspiration, which will carry us up to the crown of virtues on the keystone of the arch. In the very center of this chamber is the crystal bed, which symbolizes the transparent, translucent nature of love. The door to the grotto is of bronze and cannot be forced, but opens only to love. In this and like manner, Gottfried interprets every single detail of the structure, even to the individual parts of the door mechanism. The inside of the cave is illumined by the sun, "that blessed radiance Honor" (17,067; p. 265), shining through the three windows of Kindness, Humility, and Breeding.

The manner in which the details of the grotto are explained by Gottfried is derived from the method by which church writers exemplified the Christian truths through reference to the structure of the church; that is, they explained the details of the physical structure as symbolic of individual aspects of the Christian dogma. This in itself is notable, but it must not be assumed that Gottfried sought to represent the grotto as an allegory of Christian love, or that the lovers are there to worship at Love's altar and exemplify the tenets of their belief. Gottfried concludes his exposition with the statement that he knows this place well, having been there not once but many times, although it was never granted him to dwell there. And then he adds: "Yet I never set foot in Cornwall" (17,138; p. 266). A more striking statement of the symbolic nature of the grotto can hardly be imagined. Not only are the details of the grotto an allegory, the grotto itself is pure allegory; it is not limited in time and space.

We are, therefore, justified in looking further than the allegorical intepretation of the church structure for the meaning of the grotto and may consider the lovers' journey and their sojourn there in wider terms. We must go beyond the allegorical exegetical method to the tropological interpretation of the church as symbolizing the dwelling of God in man, the inner tabernacle in which the spirit of God resides in each individual.

It is not every individual that responds to the presence of God's spirit; not every soul seeks to effect a union with the divine spirit which is within. It is above all the goal of the mystic to attain this state of absolute union with the universal God, and it is to allegories of this experience that we must relate the grotto episode. The most obvious parallel is the much-disputed but very zealously discussed and influential interpretation of the Song of Solomon. This moving and sensuous love poetry was chiefly viewed as an allegory of the yearning of the Church (ecclesia) for union with Christ, the Church itself being often represented by its foremost member, the Virgin Mary. On an individual level, this work was seen as an allegory of the soul's passionate desire and search for ultimate union with the godhead.

Viewed in this light, it becomes clear that the progress of Tristan and Isolde toward the grotto is both an allegory of their outward existence and a symbol of their inner life. The grotto was known to Tristan, who came there earlier by chance; and although it is not specifically stated, it is to be assumed that his discovery of the grotto at a time when it did not signify anything to him means that he is destined to return there in the fullness of time. The path which brings the lovers there is a difficult one, since it passes through waste and dangerous terrain. This signifies both the hostile nature of the world in which they live and the difficulties and dangers which beset those who search inwardly for truth. This is the path which Tristan and Isolde have followed. From the moment of their illumination—following the drinking of the love potion—they have accepted the external situation which has been imposed upon them and the suffering it entailed. They have resisted every effort to destroy their relationship and sought, instead, to maintain it by accepting, with equal gladness, the moments both of joy and suffering. They have withdrawn from the world and its obligations and have concentrated their being within themselves and each other.

The grotto, which exists for Gottfried only as a symbol, is for Tristan and Isolde both a physical habitation and a symbol; it is the projection of their inner state. In this connection it is significant that Gottfried uses the word kluse (retreat or hermitage) four times to designate the grotto.[4] This word has undeniable and unmistakable associations with religion and mysticism. It is the word used for the actual place to which the ascetic retires in order to cut himself off from the world and live entirely in the spirit preparatory to the hoped-for mystical experience, the union with God. It is a word used also for the innermost secluded part of the heart or even for the womb. Tristan and Isolde are, therefore, withdrawing into themselves, concentrating their spirit only on their love and on each other, until they achieve that spiritual consummation, the complete absorption in and with the other which, in the Christian religious sphere, is identical with the union with God.

The description of the *locus amoenus* in which the grotto is situated is very detailed but, nevertheless, largely composed of typical elements. The picture contrasts markedly with the description of the May festival at Tintagel where, it will be recalled, the whole landscape was populated and where nature served as a setting for a variety of activities all more or less frivolous and pointless, mere pastimes in fact. The impression was that of an almost boisterous nature participating in the fun; and there was, without doubt, an element of irony in this picture, best summed up in the phrase: "Summer too showed clearly that he wished to keep Mark company" (676–77; p. 50).

The role of nature in the grotto—or perhaps more accurately, the role of the human element in nature—is quite different. The scene is described not once but three times; and there is a progression from the first simple description of the locality through its function as a background for their pleasure and as their court to the last passionate description, where the whole of nature surrounds them, welcoming and almost worshiping them.

We have said that this setting is a topos, and as such it has a long history. One of its most significant predecessors is the garden of pleasure into which God places Adam and Eve; and there can be no doubt that Gottfried is here drawing a deliberate parallel. By so doing, he not only associates the lovers with the parents of mankind, thereby reducing the importance of their individuality so that they become archetypal man and woman, but he also imputes to their condition a state of sinlessness; for this is the state before the Fall. They are completely one with each other and with nature and need only the presence of the other in order to remain alive. Love is all their sustenance.

"What better food could they have for body or soul? Man was there with Woman, Woman there with Man. What else should they be needing? They had what they were meant to have, they had reached the goal of their desire" (16,902–8; p. 263).

In contrast to Adam and Eve, who were provided with abundant food, Tristan and Isolde have no need of food. If they hunt, it is for amusement only, and the dog is trained to make no noise that would disturb the surroundings. It is another of the qualities attributed to mystic experience that, as long as it lasts, the body is relieved of the necessity of physical sustenance. In fact, every reference to corporeal matters, even to the physical relationship between the lovers, is strictly avoided by Gottfried. Although their bodily union is self-evidently a precondition for their state of spiritual union, it is entirely left out of the picture in favor of the spiritual relationship. This comparison with the situation of Adam and Eve in the paradise of pleasure should not be pursued too far, but it is essential not to overlook the resemblance, for at a later date the downfall of the lovers takes place in just such a garden and is then directly compared with the Fall of Man.

In this episode of the love grotto, Gottfried makes use of established Christian practices to express a belief in the power and value of love which is truly astonishing. Given a true acceptance of love and the preparedness to accept also the hardship and suffering which love entails; given the spirit to believe in the necessity of this suffering as a means of reaching a fuller experience—the lovers can finally achieve a mystic union which Gottfried can only compare with that of the Christian mystic who casts off the restrictions of the world and the flesh to attain blissful union with the Godhead. And yet there is one aspect of this experience which must not be overlooked: it can never be more than momentary. Only if we realize this fact does the return of Tristan and Isolde into society become fully understandable.

III *The Return to the World—the End*

The arrival of Mark is, of course, the end of the idyll and a reintroduction of the grossness of the normal world. Significantly, Mark is unable to catch the white stag which belongs to the world of the grotto and which presumably represents,

in some way, the perfection which he is incapable of com-
prehending. He has invaded the borders of the lovers' world,
and when they hear the sounds of hunting they retreat into
the grotto itself. This interruption follows immediately upon
the most intense description of the beauty of nature and their
harmonious union with it, but although they seclude themselves,
they are, once more, already in touch with the outside world
and its mode of life. They revert to the practice of deceit by
lying down with the naked sword between them and, in so
doing, involve themselves again in worldly behavior.

When the lovers are seen by the huntsman, he is so amazed
by the beauty of Isolde that he questions her being mortal.
She is still transfigured, radiant with illumination. With the
arrival of Mark, the emphasis changes, for he sees only her
physical beauty, the beauty of the body: "Her beauty lured his
senses to her body and the passion she excited" (17,596–98; p.
273). She is again referred to as the sun, and her beauty matches
and is enhanced by the sun shining upon her. But this light,
which shines down into the grotto and had previously been
called the light of honor, becomes now associated with the heat
of passion rather than with spiritual radiance; and the degradation of the image is symbolized by Mark's blocking this light
in order to prevent the sun harming her—who is radiance
herself—in order to preserve her beauty untouched for himself.

Gottfried dwells at length on the nature of the passion which
is aroused in Mark and, in fact, as we now pass rapidly from
the climax to the catastrophe, the poet intervenes more and
more frequently, evidencing the nature and degree of his commitment. Although Mark knows full well that Isolde is not
for him, he is determined to regain possession of her without
regard for the deeper problem. Even the King's councilors, who
are called in to hear his statement, are impressed by what they
perceive, not by what they hear from him. Mark tells them
what he had seen in the grotto and that he is *"no longer willing*
to believe that Isolde has misconducted herself in the past"
(17,668–69; p. 274). Whether or not this impresses his followers,
it is clear that they perceive what he wants and consequently
act wisely in agreeing to the recall of Isolde and Tristan to
court.

Tristan and Isolde, who had never entirely broken off relations

with the world—for their representatives Brangane and Curvenal
were always there holding, as it were, a watching brief—are
invited to return and do so without apparent reluctance. On
the superficial level, they are bound to return to society, for an
individual—at least in medieval society—was otherwise without
meaning or a center. A man existed, one might say, only
insofar as he had a reputation and could catch the echo of
himself in the world. "They would not have given anything
for a better life—save only in respect of their honor"
(16,875-77; p. 263), says Gottfried during their sojourn in
the grotto. But in a deeper sense, too, they were bound to
return. The state of ecstasy cannot be maintained indefinitely,
but must be followed by a return to the normal. This is the
experience of the mystic, for whom the world becomes then
less tolerable; for having once had the experience he longs to
renew it, or, if this is impossible, to experience the final, irrevocable consummation when the spirit leaves the body entirely.

The situation following the return of Tristan and Isolde to
court is, therefore, an intolerable one. The lovers make no
secret of their love (they cannot any longer do so), while Mark
deliberately blinds himself to their love in order not to have
to relinquish his claim. And yet he has them watched at every
turn to prevent what he does not believe exists! This is the
situation which Gottfried exposes in the bluntest of terms, calling
it a life without honor, and laying the blame fully on Mark.
The continual surveillance and enforced estrangement from
her lover make Isolde impatient for physical union with Tristan,
and in giving way to this desire, infected by Mark's attitude,
she brings about the catastrophe.

The scene is again the orchard, and in this setting the motifs
of the grotto episode and the dream of Marjodo combine with
the motifs of light and shade. In the grotto episode, everything
had been done to reduce the knowledge of physical union;
desire had not been sublimated but suspended. Here in this
final scene, it is deliberately emphasized. It is midday, and the
heat of the sun is linked with Isolde's passionate desire. The
sun which had illumined the grotto now shines "strongly, alas,
upon their honor" (18,127-28; p. 279). To cool this passion
Isolde has a bed made in the shade, which is to be a help and a
concealment, but which is not to prove secret enough. The

bed is prepared in detail and recalls the description of the bed in Marjodo's dream: "The bed and the linen which belongs to the King's bed" (13,533–34; p. 220) and "Kingly bed linen was laid in plenty on the bed" (18,150–51; p. 280). The fact that it is the King's bed and the sumptuous details contrast strongly with the simplicity and cool purity of the smooth crystal bed in the grotto. On this bed Isolde lies clad only in a shift. When the King comes upon them this time, there is no sword between them. On the contrary, they are so closely enfolded in each other's arms that a statue could not have been cast to fit together more cunningly. The final remark that they are sleeping after some exertion or other almost exactly parallels in effect and phraseology, though not in content, the situation when the King found them sleeping apart in the grotto.[5]

This, then, is their Fall; but why do they fall and what does it mean? Gottfried has prefaced this scene with an analysis of the Fall of Eve, in the course of which he makes the daring and somewhat untheological assertion that Eve would not have eaten of the fruit if God had not forbidden it. To Isolde this fruit had always been forbidden, and since the sojourn in the grotto the only change had been stricter surveillance. What has changed her attitude? In part, of course, the Fall is a direct reaction to the prohibition of their relationship, as Gottfried points out in the course of his lengthy diatribe against those who are distrustful.

Since Mark now deliberately blinds himself, there can be no hope that things will improve. But the deeper answer lies, we feel, in the experience of the grotto. They returned, says Gottfried, "but never again in all their days were they so close and familiar as they had been" (17,702–4; p. 274). In the grotto they experienced the ecstasy of complete union with the beloved and are therefore subsequently less patient with worldly restrictions. The harsher the restrictions, the more violent and unpremeditated the reaction, but—and this is the tragic element—they take the wrong path. They react against the enforced physical separation and instead of nurturing their spiritual love attempt to come together physically and openly—it is significant that their secret love is now revealed in broad daylight, whereas all other scenes had taken place at night—thereby betraying the true nature of their relationship. Through their error, they

are separated and can never meet again, but can only maintain
in isolation the purely spiritual association which will unite
them until death.

This unity is succinctly expressed in the speeches of the
lovers at parting, as they regain their senses and come to a
realization of what they have done. Tristan speaks first, begging
that Isolde never dismiss him from her heart as she will never
leave his. Isolde develops and extends this theme by saying
that nothing living—no other life—will ever find a place in her
heart but Tristan. She then goes further and stresses the
indissolubility of their union by asking him to care for himself,
since he is her life and if he dies, she, who only lives in him,
will also die: "We are one life and one flesh" (18,344; p. 282).

Isolde then ponders this thought in her long monologue
after Tristan's departure. She analyzes the conflict of emotions
within her and the insoluble nature of the problem which faces
her. She is separated from herself since she has gone with
Tristan and is yet still in Cornwall; and she is unable to find
herself. Without him she is not complete and thus lives a living
death, which is a burden and a sorrow. But Tristan, too, is
sorrowing as much as, if not more, than she; and thus she does
not bear her sorrow alone. Even in sorrow they are not separated.
So selfish and selfless is her love that she is happy that Tristan
has gone, since he has thereby saved his own, and in himself,
her life. She would rather that they lived in separation and
sorrow than that he should die for her sake by staying in
Cornwall.

Exactly how Gottfried would have completed his work we
cannot know. He would most certainly have described the
marriage of Tristan with Isolde Whitehand and presumably
also something of Tristan's later adventures. We believe that
the clandestine visits of Tristan to Isolde would, in all probability,
have been much curtailed by him in comparison with other
poets, but conjecture on this point is meaningless for interpretation. We would not like to go further than to make the following
claim. From the portrayal of Tristan's relationship to Isolde
Whitehand it is evident that Gottfried was greatly concerned
with the problem of maintaining the love relationship despite
separation. Whereas Isolde of Ireland had given way to passion
and led Tristan into error, Tristan is now guilty in exile of

falling into an error as great but more intellectually conditioned.

With great perceptiveness Gottfried portrays Tristan's progress along the path of self-deception to the point where he is able to justify to himself his marriage to the second Isolde and the betrayal of his love to the first. The marriage would have been performed but not consummated; Tristan would have stopped short of the ultimate betrayal and experienced a reversal of spirit. Unable to go through with the marriage, that is, to replace Isolde with a living substitute, he would have turned to the construction of an artificial image of the first Isolde to which he might cling. At this point, fascinating perspectives open up for a psychological interpretation of the Hall of Statues,[6] but it is precisely at this point that we must cease to interpret a work which has not been completed and turn, instead, to the conclusion of the poem, to the death of Tristan and Isolde; for although the end is not narrated, it is a *sine qua non* of the legend and has been predicted earlier by the poet.

The question of the relationship between love and death has become the most vexed aspect of the Tristan legend, not because of what Gottfried has written or not written, but because modern attitudes are much influenced by Romantic and post-Romantic Wagnerian notions. These must be firmly dismissed from the mind before considering Gottfried's veiled pronouncements on the subject.

To begin with, there is the question of Tristan's destiny as determined by the life and death of his parents. This has been discussed above, and only the essential points need be repeated here. Tristan is the physical cause of his mother's death, but she in fact owes her life to death, in return for having earlier restored Rivalin to life. Tristan is so named because the circumstances attending his birth were sad and he is thereby destined to know sadness and suffering in his own life. Specifically, Gottfried says: "See what a sorrowful life he was given to live, see the sorrowful death that brought his anguish to a close with an end beyond comparison of all deaths, more bitter than all sorrow" (2011–17; p. 68). And, as if to re-emphasize the life rather than the death, he adds: "All who have read this tale know that the name accorded with his life" (2018–20; p. 68). There is no reference to Tristan's being marked for any special death or for possessing a longing for death. His destiny is circumscribed within the terms *liebe* and *leid* (love and sorrow).

What is Tristan's own attitude to death? And how does he face it? His first serious encounter is with Morgan, where no mention is made of the risks involved. It is not until his battle with Morold that the question of death arises, and here Tristan strikes the typical attitude of the knight by maintaining that death is preferable to a life which is dishonored; that if he dies, nothing will be lost that is not already lost. The same attitude obtains on both his trips to Ireland. In the first instance, he considers the possibility of sudden death to be far preferable to the lingering death he is suffering from the poisoned wound. On his second venture, he is, of course, taking the risk on behalf of King Mark; and he again adopts the appropriate attitude, this time claiming that the risk is worth it, for even if he and all the others should die and Mark should gain Isolde, "little harm would be done" (8577; p. 154). This pose is not very convincingly maintained in view of the fact that their death could only result from the failure of their mission, and that Mark would not thereby have gained Isolde. We must assume that this bravado is directed also at the barons who reluctantly accompany Tristan and who must be listening with consternation to his devil-may-care statements. It must not be forgotten that it was, in fact, Tristan who, out of fear for his own life, persuaded Mark to agree to look for a wife.

On these occasions, the statements of Tristan have been made before entering battle, and it is instructive to note that henceforth no statements of this nature are made, although he has other battles and successes. In the battles with the dragon and with Urgan, Tristan is forced to flee to save his life and is saved on the one occasion by the dragon's loss of blood and consequent weakening and on the other by Urgan's temporary withdrawal from the fight to seek herbs. Similarly, in the bath scene Tristan pleads for his life without any show of bravado and certainly no signs of feeling that his death would be a just retribution for the killing of Morold. As an example of Tristan's concern for his own safety, we must also note that when he and Isolde withdraw to the grotto he is sufficiently cautious to have it given out that they have gone to Ireland

and to instruct Curveval to remain at court and gather information about any plot which Mark might hatch against their lives.
Also when the lovers are finally discovered by the King, Tristan
is convinced that he must escape or die. There is no suggestion
of either braving the situation or even waiting to discover the
outcome.

In all of these instances, there is no utterance which directly
impinges on the problem of death and its relation to life. Only
twice does Tristan make passing reference to the fear of death
in general. In the first instance, he excuses his slaying of Morold
as having been forced on him, since otherwise he would
have risked losing his own life, and no man willingly submits
to death. In the second instance, he warns Isolde against Mark
and Melot, comparing them to dangers against which one
should protect one's self as one says a prayer against sudden
death. On only one occasion does the deeper problem seem to
loom on the horizon, but it is then entirely dismissed and
brushed aside by Tristan. This occurs in the course of the
episode of the love potion, to which we must now turn in some
detail.

When Brangane realizes that Tristan and Isolde have drunk
the potion, she exclaims: "This drink will be the death of you
both" (11,706; p. 195). The flask itself and the drink which
it contains are referred to by her as "fatal," an adjective also
applied to the whole voyage. In the German, the word used,
veige, has the double meaning of death-bringing and destined
to die. When Brangane later explains the situation to Tristan
and Isolde, repeating the same phrase—"this drink will be the
death of you both" (12,489; p. 205)—Tristan exclaims: "Whether
it be life or death, it has poisoned me most sweetly. *I have no
idea what the other death will be like,* but this death suits me
well. If my adorable Isolde were to go on being the death of me
in this fashion, I would woo death everlasting" (12,495–502;
p. 206). This cannot but mean that Tristan fully accepts what
the potion has brought him, and that he is prepared to enjoy
and suffer love, if need be for ever. He accepts the concentration
of his life upon his beloved to the exclusion of all else. There
is no suggestion of any desire for anything beyond the enjoyment
of love in this life. Tristan entirely dismisses the real death of
the body.

To Brangane, who is concerned about the practical consequences of her mistake, the potion may seem to mean death,
for they *must* love yet *may not*. If they do not come together,
they will die; and if they do come together, they risk death
for treasonable behavior. But this is not at all the meaning
of the potion, as is very evident from Gottfried's words when
describing the effect of the drink upon those who partake
of it: "They would share one death and one life, one sorrow
and one joy" (11,443–44; p. 192). The emphasis, here as elsewhere, is on the oneness of experience, the total immersion of
the lovers in each other. They cannot continue to live except in
each other and cannot be divorced from each other, and thus
they are different from King Mark, of whom it is later said
that he lived a living death. Deprived of Isolde and knowing
it, *he* lived on as an empty shell. Neither Tristan nor Isolde *can*
live without the other, but they are not by reason of this in
any way in love with easeful death, even if they are physically
separated. They make their decision to love and accept the
ensuing burden, the joy and sorrow throughout life. Their life
and death are, at first, in the hands of Brangane, for it is she
who prevents the consummation of their love. She resigns herself,
however, and says—repeating Tristan's words (12,117–18; p. 201)
—"Let me entrust to you now, in your own keeping, your life
and your death" (12,150–51; p. 201).

Gottfried has subtly transcended the older version of the
potion, which was accidentally drunk and as a result of which
the lovers would literally die if separated. Tristan and Isolde,
although they drink the love potion by chance, nevertheless
affirm their acceptance of it, that is to say they make it *ex post
facto* their conscious choice. This is emphasized by Brangane's
words as quoted above. On the other hand, it is not separation
which threatens their life, but the non-consummation of their
love. Once this has been achieved, the seal is set on their union
and, henceforth, they cannot die even if separated; they share
one life and will share one death. From now on their life is
dedicated to the fulfillment of their love, and this love is
portrayed by Gottfried as an experience which transcends all
other worldly experience, raising the lovers to a state of
spiritual exaltation which can only be expressed in terms of
mystical religious experience.

But this experience is quite distinct from that of the religious mystic who seeks to bridge the gulf between his human corporeality, which divides him from the divine, and the God-head. The mystic is separated from God by life, by the flesh, and he attempts to achieve in his lifetime a momentary knowledge of the ineffable experience which will be permanent after the death of the body. The love of Tristan and Isolde is not for the divine but for the human element, for the other self. Their union may be termed spiritual or mystical inasmuch as they seek the union of their souls through concentration on the spirit, but it partakes of the divine only insofar as every human soul contains a spark of the divine.

For all its spirituality, the love of Tristan and Isolde is a worldly love, but an experience which gives them an inkling of the divinity of man, that is to say, permits them an experience akin to that of the religious mystic and one that can only be expressed in similar terms. This naturally raises the question of the extent to which Gottfried's "religion of love" conflicts with or supersedes the Christian view of love. Christianity, the religion of love, stresses the love relationship between Man and God or the selfless love of Man for his fellow creature as an expression of the love of God for Man. Gottfried ignores all this, as he ignores any positive reference to religious ideals and institutions, in order to stress the blissful nature of the experience of complete physical and spiritual union obtained by man and woman in this world. This is, as it were, a worldly counterpart to the religious experience, but there is no reason to assume that the experience is precluded from remaining within the Christian framework. On the contrary, we believe that the very use of the forms of Christian mysticism indicates the inclusion of this philosophy within the divine order.

Final proof of Gottfried's standpoint *vis-à-vis* the Christian religion cannot be fully established in the absence of the conclusion of the poem; for the whole problem hinges, in the final analysis, on his attitude to death. It is our view that Gottfried's religion of love lays prime emphasis on the experience to be achieved in this world as a worldly counterpart to the religious experience, which is primarily oriented toward the world hereafter. For this reason, Tristan and Isolde preserve their life as long as they can, knowing that at the end they will die together.

There is no indication that their love will then transcend death, just as there is no death wish which would presumably have been present had this been the case. The lovers will live and die as one; they will die united, but there is and could be no suggestion that death is for them the threshold of continued and transcended love experience.

IV The Poet and His Message

At the beginning of our interpretation, we indicated that the problems of finding a basis for the interpretation of a medieval work are numerous, and that not the least was the distinction between the desire of an author to be understood and the contemporary understanding of his work. To this question we must now return, for, although we have expressed our view of the meaning of the work, we must also consider the "message"—to use an unpopular term—which Gottfried wished to convey to his audience, and this naturally includes a consideration of the public to which this message was directed. In order to begin more logically with the latter point, we must turn to the prologue, in which Gottfried first establishes a relationship with his audience. This passage is sufficiently important to be quoted *in extenso:*

If I spend my time in vain, ripe for living as I am, my part in society will continue to fall short of what my experience requires of me. Thus I have undertaken a labor to please the polite world and solace noble hearts—those hearts which I hold in affection, that world which lies open to my heart. I do not mean the world of the many who . . . are unable to endure sorrow and wish only to revel in bliss. . . . What I have to say does not concern that world and such a way of life; their way and mine diverge sharply. I have another world in mind which together in one heart bears its bitter-sweet, its dear sorrow, its heart's joy, its love's pain, its dear life, its sorrowful death, its dear death, its sorrowful life (41–63; p. 42).

In the first place, it is not necessary to assume, as has sometimes been done, that Gottfried does not want, or does not expect, his work to be read by any but those to whom he specifically addresses himself. He merely states that the labor he has undertaken is for the sake of those among whom he numbers himself. He is writing for those who, like Tristan and Isolde, understand that in life and love, joy and sorrow are inextricably commingled, that life and love cannot be understood or appreciated unless these two are fully accepted. Only those who have grasped this will understand the full meaning of his work and find solace in it. Since they experience joy and suffering, they will find comfort in his work, and especially lovers; for those who suffer the pleasures and pangs of love will be both comforted and inspired by reading of others' joys and torments. Gottfried's work would, then, naturally be "caviare to the general," but he must have expected it to be read also by those who did not fully understand it. Indeed, there is a certain irony in the fact that those who read the work without great depth of understanding will not have perceived that they were being satirized.[7]

It would certainly also be wrong to see in the world to which Gottfried particularly addresses himself and of which he counts himself a member, an organized and esoteric group, a religious society or sect, or even a select few recognizable within society. In the first place, the possible audience was restricted to what would now be called the "upper classes," including the aristocracy both ecclesiastical and lay. The so-called masses did not exist as an audience for courtly works and certainly not for a man like Gottfried. Gottfried speaks to the "man of leisure," the educated and experienced man of the world. What exactly he has in mind, we shall discuss later in more detail. For the moment it is important to consider first the majority which Gottfried satirizes and rejects and which must nevertheless have also formed a part—and presumably a major part—of his actual audience. This majority consists of—to use modern terminology —the pleasure-seeking crowd, the average, unthinking man.

The only large "class" which existed and which counted was, of course, the knightly class, and it is of the typical members of this class that Gottfried is thinking. They spent their time in hunting and hawking, in feuding and tourneying, in arranging pageants and banquets, in administering the affairs of state or their own estates as best they could and often without enthusiasm. This would be a common view of the function of knighthood, despite the imposing list of duties which they swore to undertake on receiving the accolade. In this work, Gottfried portrays knights as either courageous failures or poltroons. The only exception is Tristan, and he, as we shall see, breaks every rule in the book. Rivalin is a perfect example of chivalry, but one who "over-indulged himself in pleasures dear to his heart and did entirely as he pleased" (262–64; p. 45), who "lived for the sake of living" (304; p. 46). The results of his rash behavior are—after the initial success against Morgan—catastrophic. He rushes to the aid of Mark and is severely wounded. Later he is killed by the man whom he had previously attacked on pretext and defeated. Gottfried disposes of him somewhat cynically, indicating by the manner in which his demise is portrayed that this was no very great loss: "It has come to pass, it has to be: the good Rivalin is dead. No more is required of them [his followers] than to pay the dues of a dead man, for there is nothing else to be done" (1703–9; p. 63).

Rivalin's counterpart is Mark who represents the inactive type, in contrast to the overly active Rivalin. Mark is an example of the *roi-fainéant* but without the redeeming strength of character that enabled King Arthur to make his court a veritable center of chivalry. His early submission to Ireland is excused as the result of his minority; but by or even before the time Rivalin arrives there, he is clearly of age and has undertaken nothing. When Rivalin arrives, he is arranging a splendid pageant. It is not said to what extent Mark participates in the campaign in which Rivalin is wounded. Later, when Tristan comes to the court, Mark is so impressed by his qualities that he entreats him to stay, not as a knight, but rather as a courtier—"you can do everything I want"—and becomes to a large degree dependent for his pleasures on Tristan.

The arrival of Morold throws the whole court into a panic and no one—least of all apparently Mark—is willing to risk his life. They all prefer, as Tristan points out, a dishonored life (having bartered their children to save it) to the risk of death, but at least an honorable death. These same knights are later portrayed as being terrified by Tristan's proposal to take them with him to Ireland and yet cunning enough to advise the King in order to obtain their own ends—to displace Tristan—and later to maintain their popularity by recommending him to recall Isolde from the grotto. Yet by these and others, such as the dwarf Melot, the King is persuaded first one way and then another. If Rivalin was headstrong, self-willed, and rash, he at least made decisions and attempted to carry them out boldly. Mark seems devoid of any strength of character. His true nature is gradually exposed as he becomes more and more involved in the relationship with Tristan and Isolde.

The most striking evidence of Gottfried's attitude toward knighthood, its pomp and circumstance and the disparity between theory and practice, is contained in the description of the knighting of Tristan. Gottfried begins this passage in a stereotyped manner with a complaint of his inability to do justice to the description of such a ceremony, and instead of making the attempt, he does not describe the ceremony, but instead provides his audience with a short history of the literature of the past two generations. This and the following bombastic outline of how he would describe Tristan's preparations if he could—liberally larded, as it is, with references to classical mythology—must have been largely unintelligible to all but the most educated minority. But the more galling aspect is surely the sovereign artistry which he displays and which so obviously would have enabled him to describe the ceremony he so pointedly claims to be unable to describe.

The greater irony lies, however, in the definition of the aims of knighthood which Gottfried, nevertheless, introduces at the close of this passage. Mark, the weak and pleasure-loving Mark, advises Tristan: "Be modest and straightforward. Be truthful and well-bred. Always be kind to the poor; to the rich always be proud. Cultivate your appearance. Honor and love all women. Be generous and loyal and never tire of it . . ." (5027–36; p. 110). The irony of this counsel lies not so much in the fact that the audience knows full well what kind of relationship will develop between Mark and Tristan, but in the fact that Tristan proceeds to discard every one of these honorable precepts in the action to follow. His modesty is rarely in evidence except as a form of mock modesty, as he willingly allows his talents to be drawn out and displayed. He is rarely straightforward, preferring, at all times, to tell untruths in order to gain advantage. The precept of honoring and loving all women he has no chance to put into practice, since he is never in a situation to help anyone but Isolde in defeating the steward. Certainly his behavior toward

his uncle's wife and his later treatment of Isolde Whitehand
accord ill with his oath. Tristan maintains or discards his loyalty
at will.

As an example of the subtlety with which Tristan, with little
or no consideration for veracity, turns every situation to his
advantage, let us consider the passage in which—after all the
untruths he has been telling come to light through the discovery
of the damaged sword—he explains to Queen Isolde and her
daughter his mission to Ireland:

After my first voyage here, when I was cured, I sang your praises
continually to my Lord Mark, till my prompting turned his thoughts
so strongly toward you that he summoned the resolution for the deed,
but only just, and I will tell you why. He feared your enmity, and
in any case wished to stay single for my sake, so that I could succeed
him when he died. But I urged him against it until he began to give
way to me (10, 551–66; p. 180).

This is a very subtle but nonetheless distinct distortion of
the truth. Tristan had begged Mark to marry only because he
feared for his own life, and Mark gave way only because
Tristan threatened otherwise to leave him. The King, then, chose
Isolde partly because she had been praised by Tristan but
primarily because he thought this would make a marriage impossible—hardly a flattering thought for Isolde! As Tristan puts
it, it not only sounds better to the Isoldes, he also displays
himself in an advantageous light. On other occasions—to mention
a few only in passing—Tristan cuts down Morgan without warning (having concealed his weapon under his cloak) and takes
advantage of Morold's temporary weakness to cripple him and
then pours scorn on his helpless adversary. He also takes advantage of a friendly and not seriously intended offer on the
part of his friend Gilan, in order to extort from him his favorite
dog in precisely the same manner in which Gandin had tricked
Mark out of Isolde. On that occasion Tristan had had hard words
for his uncle.

Tristan is, in other words, always successful, not merely as
an artist, but equally in his prowess as a knight. His success
sets him apart from the average knight and indicates the difference in quality between the world to which he belongs and
the average world, *"ir aller werlt."* The average man, either
ineffectually engaged in mundane matters or engrossed in the

pursuit of amusement and the pleasures of the body, is surpassed in every way by this *elite*, even in those areas which have no great meaning for them. To a certain extent, this superiority may be said to be an innate gift, something not to be acquired by everyone; but in large measure it is also the result of early, intense, and continued cultivation of mind and spirit. Such training does not make one less able to function on the lower level. On the contrary, it endows one with superior abilities in wordly matters but deprives one of interest in them. It is at this point that we must return to the question of education.

Gottfried lays great emphasis on Tristan's education (2056ff.; p. 68), which comprised instruction in the arts, specifically languages, literature, and music. Perhaps it is significant that Gottfried says "that in addition to these" (2103; p. 69)—thereby placing the others in perspective?—he learned the chivalric accomplishments of riding, fencing, hunting, and so forth. Although the beginning of his studies is called "the beginning of his cares" (2086; p. 68), yet there is no suggestion of deprivation. On the contrary, it is clearly understood that, once in the ban of these studies, Tristan developed an inborn propensity to the very highest level. In turn, Tristan instructs Isolde in the arts which he has acquired, although, of course, in this case the instruction is restricted specifically to the finer arts of language, literature, and music. She too had had an excellent education even before his arrival, but it was still inadequate. Under Tristan's tutelage she develops her innate talents with great rapidity to a level of accomplishment that astonishes the world.

In particular Gottfried speaks of *"moraliteit,"* a term that has stirred up considerable discussion. This study is defined by Gottfried as "a good and wholesome thing. Its teaching is in harmony with God and the world. In its precepts it bids us to please both, and it is given to all noble hearts as a nurse, for them to seek in her doctrine their life and their sustenance" (8009–017; p. 147). This rather vague definition of the French term *moralité*—defined in the Old French dictionary as *bon sens*—seems to mean the art of maintaining always and in every situation an amiable disposition, a pleasing and winning way, of adopting an attitude that will maintain one's honor and win one esteem, no matter how difficult or desperate the situation. The "morality" of this may be questionable, but it seems to sug-

gest that faculty by means of which the *elite* of which Gottfried
speaks remains perfectly in control of any situation and pleasing
to God and man—in which there is presumably no religious im-
plication. This is the quality which enables Tristan and Isolde
to carry through and carry off their various deceits without
prejudice either to their reputation at court or their conviction
of being in the right.

That Mark does not belong to this world is only too evident.
He represents an inferior world, and his nature unfolds itself
in the course of the conflict for the possession of Isolde, who
stands between Tristan and Mark, bound to the one by genuine
love and to the other by the moral, social, and legal code. At
first, Mark is too gross to notice the difference between Brangane
and Isolde. Later he is too engrossed in physical possession to
perceive that Isolde loves his nephew. Persuaded now by his
enemies, now by the lovers, he vacillates between suspicion of
their guilt and implicit belief in their innocence. When he finally
begins to suspect on his own account, he can only turn from
private to public advisers, demonstrating his complete inability
to appreciate the nature of love. But up to this point, and then
through the ordeal episode, Gottfried does not outrightly condemn his behavior, but rather exposes it as pitiful. Mark's guilt
does not really begin to grow until after the lovers have returned
from the grotto.

Mark's determination to regain Isolde is motivated entirely
by physical desire and not by any genuine belief in her innocence.
Although this is not expressly stated, it is implied by the attitude
of his councilors who fall in with his obvious desire to have
Isolde back without being convinced by the reason which is
given. The hypocrisy which Gottfried condemns in Mark lies
in his setting spies to hinder a love which he publicly claims
does not exist. He pretends blindness which—says Gottfried—
comes from purely sensual lust and passion. The meaning of
the scenes following the return from the grotto is very fully
explained by Gottfried in his lengthy sermon based on the text:
"A virtuous woman needs no guardian." His argument is basically that the distrust which leads to the surveillance of an honest
woman breeds distrust in her, to the extent of driving her to
provide a reason for the lack of trust. In other words: prohibition breeds the crime.

Mark, of course, cannot help himself and forces the catastrophe. The tragic quality of the ensuing episode, therefore, lies in the destruction of what is great and good by inferior motives. Mark, it is true, suffers as well; and in a limited way Gottfried shows some sympathy for him. He has always tried to find the truth and has been unconvinced until, knowing the truth in his heart, he shuns it and tries to destroy it. At this point, he unintentionally finds the truth unequivocally demonstrated before his eyes, with the result that his life too is destroyed: "He no longer fancied, he knew. . . . All his past efforts to rid himself of doubt had now ended in living death" (18,222–30; p. 281). For Tristan and Isolde there is tragedy, for they are thrown off balance by the circumstances which surround them and are trapped into falling below the true level of their existence. As a result they are punished by separation, but, while they must endure love's suffering in isolation, with only a remote hope of eventual reunion, at least they have this love to sustain them; Mark has nothing.

The end would thus seem tragic in the sense that Tristan and Isolde have irrevocably lost the chance of real happiness, and nothing related after this point can alter that. The question, therefore, arises as to whether or not Gottfried viewed this kind of love as inevitably leading to conflict and tragedy, and whether he is presenting this story as a precept or as a warning. To answer these questions we must recall the words of the prologue and remember how Tristan and Isolde spent their days in the grotto. Gottfried had earlier said:

I have offered the fruits of my labor to this world as a pastime, so that with my story its denizens can bring their keen sorrow half-way to alleviation and thus abate their anguish. . . . It is a good thing that one who harbors love's pain and sorrow in his heart should seek distraction with all his mind—then his spirit will find solace and release. . . . This sorrow is so full of joy, this ill so inspiring that, having once been heartened by it, no noble heart will forego it. I know as sure as death and have learned it from this same anguish: the noble lover loves love-tales (45–122; p. 42).

Although he does not specifically say so, it must be assumed that the love tales to which Gottfried refers are tales of "tragic" love, just as his own story. Certainly when they are in the grotto, Tristan and Isolde tell each other tales of the tragic love affairs of the past even though there is at that moment no suggestion of imminent tragedy. And yet they must know that there can be no lasting fulfillment for them, for they cannot completely escape from the world with which they are in conflict, as were the lovers of whom they tell. Such love as they speak of and such love as theirs cannot, however, be destroyed, no matter how much it may be obstructed and saddened by the world. It outlasts death by being passed on to future generations. If their love does not find permanent fulfillment in life, at least they achieve momentary exaltation and maintain it undiminished into death. In their death their love, then, finds another kind of fulfillment, for it now lives on in others and provides the sustenance which enables future lovers to bear similar adversities. In this way, their love, though apparently tragic in its immediate result, triumphs over the inferiority of the world which uncomprehendingly rejects it, and it is no tragedy for those with understanding. Their life is tragic only insofar as it partakes of the tragic imperfection of the whole human race, which can never attain a perfect state or find complete fulfillment in human existence, but must always stumble and fall anew.

The conflict between the lovers and the world which Mark represents is certainly inevitable. Gottfried advocates that those who have the necessary insight into this situation should cultivate their esthetic sensibilities through literature and music and should withdraw as much as possible from mundane responsibilities. He advocates this for both man and woman so that the woman becomes an equal partner in the experience, with the right to make her own choice. But since it is Mark who represents the world as it is, the lovers' conflict with him means a clash with the existing social order. In the simplest possible terms: Gottfried is on the side of illicit love against the legal husband. How is this to be understood?

In looking at this question it is important to avoid thinking in terms of twentieth-century morality and advisable also to pass over the question of the attitude toward marriage in Gottfried's time. Rather we should look first toward the literature of Gottfried's day, and the ideals expressed there, and compare these with Gottfried's work and the views which he proffers. Of the two great forms of literature at the beginning of the thirteenth century, minnesong had as its basis the love of a man for a woman who was either his superior in life and, for that reason, unapproachable, married to another or, for some other reason, unattainable. In the most extreme case, a man could be in love with a woman he had never seen. It is true that in earlier works erotic love breaks through and reappears subsequently with Walther von der Vogelweide. In addition there was one form—the dawn song—in which the situation was always the same (the parting of lovers at dawn) and always presupposed physical union. The basic element remained, however, the cultivation of a purely spiritual love.

In the courtly epic, the other great literary form of the period, there is emphasis on action rather than contemplation, and the knight, by his prowess, wins and marries the lady. The idea of love is here completely different, for the lady is won without wooing and the result is marriage, whereas in minnesong she is always wooed but never won and the result is normally rejection, certainly never more than a form of distant encouragement. The story of Tristan might, therefore, be considered as a classic minnesong situation: the knight in love with the wife of another, her station also being above his. But Gottfried cuts right through the conventional posturing and emphasizes that their love became complete only after their physical union, while the husband, who is normally ignored in minnesong, is portrayed in detail as ignoble and essentially guilty. The relationship which is compounded by the epic situation of Tristan having in fact risked his life to "win" the lady, leads not to marriage or to courtly spiritual love but to "courtly adultery."[8]

While it is true that morality, in the sense of conventional chivalric posturing, means little to Gottfried, it is not necessary to see in the outcome of his story either a condemnation of marriage and approval of adultery or a condemnation of adultery as leading inevitably to tragedy. Nowhere in Gottfried's work is there a suggestion that love cannot lead to marriage or that it must result in tragedy, if one of the partners is already married. Tristan and Isolde are exemplary and represent the utmost limits of human endeavor both in their love and in the obstacles which it must face. Never has the world known such lovers, but never have lovers been beset by so many difficulties or persecuted by such base enemies. Although Gottfried portrays character with due respect for verisimilitude, he is nevertheless concerned to portray Mark and his supporters as representative of the worst elements of the lower world—gross sensuality, envy, and pure evil—the most complete denial of the values for which he stands. By so doing, he establishes the primacy of the love bond over the (civil) marriage bond; but this is done without intent to undermine authority, either juridical or ecclesiastical.

Tristan and Isolde are, therefore, exemplary in spirit only. A knowledge of the manner in which they nurture and maintain their love, in spite of the evil forces marshaled against them, will sustain others in their lesser suffering, in the burden of life and the torments of love; just as the mystic and the monk are uplifted and strengthened by reading the lives of saints and martyrs who have gone before them. For Gottfried, the essential thing is that the noble in spirit should preserve love from debasement by a sensual and materialistic society and should foster and spread the appreciation of the true nature of love, its supreme and eternal virtue. Should the other world refuse to recognize the existence of Gottfried's world and, in its jealousy, set about deliberately to destroy it, then the world of the spirit, the true spirit of love, should supersede the degradation of marriage which, in Gottfried's eyes, is the equivalent of purchasing a wife, of "love . . . for sale in the open market" (12,296; p. 203), whereas in truth:

> Love is so blissful a thing
> so blessed an endeavor,
> that apart from its teaching
> none attains worth or reputation. (187–90; p. 43)

CHAPTER 4

The Essential Features of Gottfried's Style

E VEN for an age which appreciated virtuosity far more than our own Gottfried's style stands out as incredibly complex; it is beyond the scope of this work to investigate all the varied elements which compose this style: his choice of words and epithets, the use of word patterns and sound patterns, rhyme, assonance, and so forth. To a large extent, such a detailed analysis would also lose most of its force without extensive quotation in the original language. In this chapter, style will, therefore, be interpreted in the wider and more general sense to mean the dominant features of Gottfried's method of presentation, the essential elements in the organization and expression of his material which give his work a character peculiarly its own. This will involve a discussion both of the larger questions of organization, that is, structure, and of more detailed features of verbal arrangement. These, rather than specific aspects of embellishment and coloring, are the elements of style relevant to an understanding of the poem.

I Over-all Structure

At various points throughout his work, Gottfried has placed initial letters which, if the poem had been completed, would have made up the names of the hero and the heroine and probably also of the author himself. As we have mentioned, each of the letters of the names Tristan and Isolde(n) appears twice within a relatively short space, the second time in reverse order. The letters of Tristan's name enclose or "embrace" those of Isolde's. These initial letters are placed as follows:

T	41	R	1791	I	5099	S	12,431	T	A	N
								(19,500)	(12,000)	(24,750)
I	45	S	1795	O	5103	L	12,435	D	E	N
I	131	S	1865	O	5177	L	12,503	D	E	N
T	135	R	1869	I	5181	S	12,507	T	A	N

The number of the lines intervening between the two pairs of letters varies, but the first letter of each pair invariably introduces a quatrain with a special rhyme scheme: the same two rhyme words are repeated (either *abba* or *abab*). The second of the two letters always follows this quatrain. If the distance between the groups of letters is reduced to an approximation, it appears that there is a pattern of progression in the number of lines, viz., 1750–3500–7000; and the remaining letter groups would presumably have occurred after a further 7000, 3500, and 1750 lines. Actually the numbers fall a little short of this calculation; and it may well be that the total would have been 24,000 rather than the 25,000 lines suggested.[1]

The length of the poem is not in itself an important point, but it has some bearing on the question of the positioning of the next (missing) group of letters: T D D T. Even by the larger calculation, this group should appear at a point which has already been reached when the poem breaks off at line 19,548. For this reason, and since we also believe that the final passages in the poem as we have it cannot be in "finished" form—there is some confusion in the order of the narrative—we contend that Gottfried would have made his next division immediately following the parting of the lovers. This would be in our text between lines 18,400 and 18,600. It is highly improbable that the development of the relationship between Tristan and Isolde Whitehand and their marriage would have been included in the section which began with the love of Tristan and Isolde. Our following analysis of the structure is, therefore, based on the assumption that the initials T D D T should have been set after the parting of the lovers; and we feel that the structure itself—as we view it—supports this premise.

Whatever the exact length of the individual sections—and it is not necessary to suppose that they would have been planned to form an exact correspondence—there is an evident proportionate relationship between them, as indicated above. The whole poem would have been divided approximately as follows:

Introduction	A	B	C	D	E	F	Conclusion
	1750	3500	7000	7000	[3500	1750]	
	T	R	I	S	T	A	N
	1 :	2 :	4 :	4.. :	2 :	1	

The material is divided into (A) the story of Tristan's parents, (B) Tristan's early life until his knighthood, (C) Tristan's life up to the time of the love potion, (D) the love of Tristan and Isolde until the time of their parting. It is, of course, impossible to say how the remainder of the work would have been organized, but we assume that the description of Tristan's early life would have been balanced by his later life in exile (B : E), while the story of his parentage and birth would have been counterbalanced by the events leading up to his death (A : F).[2]

The symmetry of this layout is not at all surprising. Its result is to place the drinking of the love potion and the first expression of their love in the exact center of the work. We have already pointed out that it may surprise the modern reader to find that Tristan and Isolde do not fall in love until halfway through the poem, but we suggested, at the same time, that there was a reason behind this, namely the author's desire to stress the inevitable fulfillment of fate, the fact that these two people, destined, as they are, for one another, are bound eventually to reach the point of union. If we look briefly at the organization of these two larger portions of the narrative, it will be seen that this idea is underlined by the contrasting tenor of the action, i.e., by the contrast between motion and stability.

The second part (B) may be reduced to Tristan's upbringing, his abduction to Cornwall, and his knighthood. Although the third part (C) begins with his trip to Parmenie, Tristan views Cornwall as his real home and returns there as soon as possible. His connection with Isolde begins, then, with the battle against Morold; for following this battle he makes his voyage to Ireland, where he acts as Isolde's tutor before returning to Cornwall. His second trip to Ireland occurs under entirely different auspices, and the two journeys parallel, in some way, his journeys from Parmenie to Cornwall. On his first passage, he had been abducted and was in despair, just as he set out in despair for Ireland when his wound proved incurable. In each case the second voyage takes place under more auspicious circumstances than the first, although in each case it is followed by a battle, first with Morold, later with the dragon.

The motif of the voyage is a very important one both for the over-all structure and for the meaning of the work. Isolde herself points to the relevance of the voyage motif—after they

have drunk the potion but before they have declared their love—
by reminding Tristan how he had first come to Ireland alone
and as a sick man. At that time, he was in search of a cure for
his sickness at the hands of the Queen. Now he is again mortally
sick—this time of love—and the only possible cure lies in the
love of the younger Isolde. The reference to the solitary man in
the small boat also recalls Tristan's battle with Morold; for he
had, at that time, boasted that only one boat would be needed
after the battle. It is he who then uses this boat; but he is
already wounded. Finally, the scene looks forward to the last
voyage, Isolde's, as she comes—too late—to heal the dying Tristan.
The relevance of this voyage is evident even though Gottfried
did not complete his work. He could not possibly have omitted
this ending.

It is unnecessary to refer in detail to the events following the
love potion in order to substantiate the contrast between these
two larger sections. Whatever the interrelationship of the episodes
preceding and following the drinking of the love potion, it is
clear that Gottfried stresses the movement—one might almost say
the instability—of Tristan's existence up to the point of his love
for Isolde. He travels (unwillingly) from Parmenie to Cornwall,
then back to Parmenie, returning again to Cornwall. Twice he
journeys to Ireland, and it is only on the second homeward voyage
that he meets his destiny. In the section following the love potion
(D), he remains with Isolde with the exception of a brief
period subsequent to the ordeal. Only when he is forced to leave
Isolde do his travels resume. If his earlier journeys unknowingly
and circuitously brought him closer to Isolde, his subsequent
efforts are directed toward motion for the sake of motion, and
action in order to sublimate sorrow.

In the second section the change of scenery, the continuous
to and fro of the earlier long section, is replaced by an emotional
fluctuation, an alternation of joy and sorrow for the lovers, and
trust and suspicion for Mark. Despite this pendulum motion,
however, there is a steady linear progression toward the climax
and a gradual widening of the circle of those involved. The
first episodes following the consummation of the love of Tristan
and Isolde—the first incidents, that is, in the development of
their conflict with society—have no direct bearing on the problems
which are eventually to lead to their separation; but they have

nevertheless a bearing on the personal relationship of the lovers to one another and to Mark.

On the wedding night, Brangane had substituted for Isolde, and Isolde soon attempts to have her murdered in order not to have anyone know of her secret. This latter part is introduced with the words: "Isolde was greatly loved and honored by her Lord, Mark" (12,675–77; p. 208) and ends with the reconciliation of Isolde with Brangane. The bridge from this to the following Gandin episode is provided by a description of the joy and sorrow experienced by the lovers under the existing circumstances, and the Gandin episode is then introduced with a description of Tristan's spirited nature, much as Isolde had been referred to before. This episode involves Tristan alone, just as the preceding one had centered around Isolde; but it ends as the first one had begun, namely with the lovers spending the night together and deceiving Mark. Whereas Tristan had previously been bound in loyalty to bring Isolde to Mark, and had agreed to the wedding-night deception and substitution, he has now won her from an admirer to whom Mark had foolishly lost her, so that the time they spend together after escaping from Gandin is, in some degree, a demonstration of his right to her. The two episodes—Brangane and Isolde, Tristan and Gandin—therefore begin and end in a similar manner and are also of approximately equal length—504 and 516 lines.

From this point on the conflict begins to grow and to involve an increasing number of persons. Brangane makes her first mistake in leaving the door open—a similar mistake leads to the final discovery—and this results in the discovery of the lovers' secret by Marjodo. Marjodo incites the King to trap Isolde but is defeated by Brangane, and the first stage ends in success for the lovers. Melot makes a similar attempt, and the result is again success for the lovers, this time largely through Tristan's watchfulness. But when the three (Mark, Melot, and Marjodo) unite in a carefully planned plot against the lovers aided by Brangane the result is inconclusive, and this leads directly to the ordeal. The ordeal may, therefore, be said to form a single episode with the blood-letting scene, so that all three episodes are of approximately the same length.

Following these episodes, there is a lengthy interpolation in Tristan's battle with Urgan, and one may wonder why this further delay has been introduced—at least in this extended form—before the climax of the grotto. It is true that the various episodes represent the trials and tribulations of the lovers before they finally reach the grotto, and the ordeal may be said to be the most acute danger. And yet the Urgan episode has a valuable function, not only for its representation of the undisturbed harmony and trust of the lovers and the utter selflessness which proves them ready for the grotto; it also provides for a passage of time before the banishment of the lovers from court. This would hardly have been credible had it followed directly on the ordeal which announced Isolde's innocence to the world. Once the climax has been reached and passed, however, as the lovers leave the grotto, Gottfried allows no major interruption before the inevitable catastrophe. This follows rapidly on the climax and concludes, we believe, the second central section.

The two major sections surrounding the center of the work are, therefore, in a sense parallel in the form of their development. In the first part, Tristan and Isolde finally come together after meeting and losing sight of one another and after numerous obstacles, which seemed to have made it impossible for them ever to come together, have been overcome. In the second part, their love must stand the test of numerous trials, and the alternation in emotion which results from them until they can finally be united in the grotto. As the consummation of their love was followed by concern for the approaching wedding night, so the grotto scene is interrupted by a summons back to reality which results, in this case, in immediate catastrophe.

II *The Structure of Individual Passages—Word-Play*

As we have seen, the whole poem is so constructed as to center on the scene in which Tristan's and Isolde's love is consummated; and preceding and following sections are symmetrically disposed. If we now look at the layout of the potion scene itself, it will be found that it, too, is largely based on this principle, which has been called bilateral symmetry.[3] The scene begins with sixty-two lines in which the situation is rapidly sketched and the action moved forward from the anchoring in the harbor through the drinking of the potion to Brangane's expression of dismay and her disposal of the fatal flask. The passage that follows on this quick narrative is devoted to an

analysis of the feelings of Tristan and Isolde and their surrender
to their feelings. At first, the situation is analyzed in general
terms; then Tristan's inner conflict with, and submission to,
love is described. Following this, there is a similar analysis of
Isolde's state of mind; this, in turn, leads to a general description
of their feelings after giving way to love. The passage is symmetrically arranged in groups of 34—48 52—34 lines.

Immediately afterwards, the line which had introduced the
scene—"the ships went on their way" (11,645; p. 194)—is picked
up in the line "the ships now put out again" (11,875; p. 198)
and the next section introduced. This second passage describes
their mutual confession of love and its consummation. It consists
of two parts of exactly one hundred and fifty-four lines each,
and there is a distinct parallelism in the progression of each part.
The first part refers to their unrest when out of sight of each
other and to their embarrassment and estrangement. Each
changes color in the presence of the other, but finally Isolde
begins to talk about the past. She recalls Tristan's first visit
as Tantris and how she had almost slain him in the bath and
how—if she had known then what she knows now—she would
not have hesitated when his life was in her hands. This passage
leads to the mutual confession of love. The second part of the
passage traces the development from the first bold look—for all
embarrassment is now gone—to the exchange of kisses. The
physical effects on the lovers are, however, now even more
serious; for they not only continue to change color, but waste
away for lack of seclusion. In the conversation which is instigated
by Brangane, they put their lives into her hands, and she lets
them have their will, so that the consummation is achieved. It
should be noted, in passing, that this passage leads up to the
fourth of the initial letters of Gottfried's name, at which point
he begins his lengthy discourse on love. At the end of the discourse, the initials S L and L S appear, between which there
occurs the scene in which Brangane explains the potion and
Tristan joyfully embraces his fate. This is, technically, the "exact"
center of the work.

❋ ❋ ❋

An analysis of the complex word-play in these scenes would be
too lengthy an undertaking; but it should be noted that the
device is used differently in the two passages. In the earlier

passage, Gottfried uses contrast to express conflict, that is, the tension between the lovers and the conflicting emotions within them. In Tristan's heart, the conflict is largely one between loyalty and love; as for Isolde, "that warring company a maid and a man, love and modesty brought her into great confusion" (11,824–26; p. 196). In the later passage, which begins with the contrast of the ships "gaily" sailing on their way and the two hearts "led astray" and "burdened" with the problem of their love, there is a parallelism in which the emotional states of the first part are overcome or superseded in the second; for example the phrase, "shyness and modesty robbed them of their joy" (11,901–2) is balanced by "their shy reserve was over" (12,037; p. 200). The type of word-play in these passages—the use of antithetical or associated word pairs and the repetition of key words in linked passages and in order to link passages—is an important element of Gottfried's style and will be discussed in more detail below. In order more fully to exemplify the type of symmetrical structure used by Gottfried, we must first look at the way in which the second major climax of the poem, the grotto episode, is contrived.

The structure of the grotto episode is an interesting example of how Gottfried links passages together by cross-reference. When, for example, Tristan and Isolde leave the court, they leave Brangane behind to watch over their interests. They also take Curvenal with them to the grotto, which is introduced to the audience in a lengthy description both of its inside appearance and its surroundings. This description is given before the lovers arrive. When they arrive, they keep the dog and send Curvenal back to court as their link with the outside world. Thus, although they are now established in the grotto, Gottfried has indicated that they are not entirely cut off from the court. At this point, the poet describes how Tristan and Isolde live in the grotto, that is, how they were nourished; and he describes at length how they had their own world and their own court in the form of nature. The purely spiritual nature of their nourishment is re-emphasized at the end of the passage before Gottfried returns to the description of the grotto.

When he does return to the question of the grotto, it is to introduce the allegorical interpretation as a deliberate interpola-

tion, beginning: "I beg you to bear with me while I explain . . ."
(16,923ff.; p. 264). This interpretation, which begins as an address
to the audience in the "you" form, leads later to a self-identifica-
tion of the author with the audience, "for *us* martyrs" (17,085;
p. 266) and ends with the author's personal experience—"I know
all this for I was there" (17,100; p. 266). Following the interpolation, Gottfried resumes his description of the lovers' life and
explains in detail their daily occupation, which includes hunting
for pastime and thus prepares the change of scene, when Mark
is setting out to hunt.

The remainder of the passage consists of a close interweaving
of the actions in the two worlds which now meet at this place.
The narration of the hunt is interrupted by the most passionate
description of Tristan's and Isolde's life in perfect harmony with
the grotto and their withdrawal into the latter on hearing the
hunt approach. After the discovery by Mark, there is a further
passage concerning the lovers and their reaction at having been
discovered, before Mark makes his decision to bring them back.
The whole episode is, therefore, closely integrated in order to
demonstrate the gradual withdrawal into the grotto and also
the continuing awareness of the existence of the outside world.
Within the grotto area itself, we notice a marked emphasis on
the unity of duality by means of continual reference to inside and
outside, the pleasure of heart and mind, the delights of nature
pleasing to eye and ear, and so forth.

The allegorical interpretation of the grotto is aimed at il-
lustrating this point and we find that its form is again bilateral.
Very briefly, it is organized as follows: Gottfried introduces his
interpretation by saying that he will explain the meaning of the
nature of the walls inside—round, broad, high, perpendicular,
smooth, snow-white, and even throughout its whole circum-
ference. This he does in the first forty-six lines and then moves
to an explanation of the floor and the bed, neither of which he
had reintroduced above. At this stage, he reiterates that the
door was bolted and latched and proceeds to a lengthy explanation of the bolts and the door. This also takes up forty-six
lines, at which point he leaves the inside of the grotto and passes
on to a description of the outside. This description is introduced
by the lines: "The secret lever of tin which had been let into

the latch *from outside* . . ." (17,031ff.; p. 265), and here there is a clear change from the internal to the external, suggested also by a division in the manuscript.

Up to this point, the description of the interior has occupied one hundred and eight lines. The following passage, which explains the meaning of the latch, the iron doors, the surrounding area, and the concluding definition of the whole as an allegory, occupies precisely the same number of lines. Of the first group of one hundred and eight lines, forty-six, as we have seen, are devoted to the walls and forty-six to the door. In between we have, therefore, the sixteen lines explaining the floor and the bed—eight lines each. The exact center of the passage is, accordingly, between the description of floor and bed, and the line introducing the second half reads: "The bed in the center . . ." (16,977; p. 264). Gottfried has thus produced an exactly symmetrical structure—46–8–8–46—which places the floor/bed interpretation in his poem as it is placed in the physical location, namely in the very center. In addition, he has balanced the number of lines devoted to the description of the inside of the grotto with an equal number for the outside.

This is but one of numerous examples of numerically symmetrical structure which could be adduced from this or other episodes in Gottfried's work; and such numerical correspondences are often very significant. But, as this example is intended to show, it is not the numbers themselves which are important but the form, the structure, and the harmonious balance they represent. This type of structure is indicative of Gottfried's amazing sense of symmetry and proportion; it should not be confused with what is often called number symbolism.[4]

The symmetrical structure referred to extends also to the use of word patterns; and, while sound patterns, which form an integral part of this complex, cannot be analyzed in translation, two passages will serve to demonstrate the extent to which Gottfried has structured smaller units in intricate patterns of meaning. These passages have been chosen at random and largely for their brevity and adaptability into English.

The first passage describes the *"moraliteit"* or *"bienséance"* which Tristan/Tantris teaches to Isolde (8002ff.; p. 147).

Among all this teaching	*teaching*	under aller dirre lere
he gave her one occupation	*occupation*	gab er ir eine unmüeze- keit,
which we call bienséance.	*bienséance*	die heizen wir moraliteit.
The art teaches fine be- havior.	*teaches*	diu kunst diu leret schoene site:
With this all ladies should		da solten alle vrouwen mite
in their youth be occupied.	*occupied*	in ir jugent unmüezic wesen.
Bienséance, that sweet study,	*bienséance*	moraliteit, daz süeze lesen
is blissful and pure.		deist saelic unde reine.
Its teaching has association	*teaching*	ir lere hat gemeine
with the world and with God.	*world & God*	mit der werlde und mit gote.
It teaches us in its commandment	*teaches*	si leret uns in ir gebote
to please God and the world.	*God & world*	got unde der werlde gevallen:
To all noble hearts		sist edelen herzen allen
it is given as a nurse		zeiner ammen gegeben,
that they their nourishment		daz si ir lipnar unde ir leben
and life seek in its teaching,	*teaching*	suochen in ir lere;
for they have prosperity nor honor		wan sin hant guot noch ere,
if they are not taught by bienséance.	*taught* *bienséance*	ezn lere si moraliteit.
This was the chief occupation	*occupation*	diz was ir meiste unmüezekeit
of the young queen.		der jungen küniginne.

The word-play in this passage is relatively simple. It consists of the rapid repetition of the words teaching/teaches/taught and the association of the key words *bienséance* and occupy/occupation. A basic principle of Gottfried's word patterns is also evident, namely the central positioning of a key concept, in this case the stress on man's relationship with the world and God. It will be noted that these words are repeated in reverse form, thus also pointing, in a manner of speaking, inward.

The second passage follows closely after the first and describes the seductive qualities of Isolde after she has mastered all that Tristan could teach her. This is a much more complex though equally short example, and an attempt has been made to illustrate the word patterns, again without entering into the matter of sound structure (8085ff.; p. 148).

English	Word pattern	Middle High German
To whom may I liken her,		Wem mag ich si gelichen
the beautiful, blissful,		die schoenen, saelderichen
but to one of the Sirens	*Sirens*	wan den Syrenen eine,
who with the lodestone	*lodestone*	die mit dem agesteine
draw ships to them.	*draw, ships*	die kiele ziehent ze sich?
So drew Isolde, it seems to me,	*drew*	als zoch Isot, so dunket mich,
many hearts and thoughts in	*hearts* *thoughts, in*	vil herzen unde gedanken in,
which yet thought themselves secure		die doch vil sicher wanden sin
from loving disquiet.		von senedem ungemache.
Also are these two things,		ouch sint die zwo sache,
ship without anchor and the mind,	*ship without anchor*	kiel ane anker unde muot
good for comparison.		zebenmazene guot:
They are so *seldom* both		si sint so selten beide
on a *steady course,*		an staeter wegeweide,
so *often* in an *uncertain harbor,*		so dicke in ungewisser habe,
tossing both up and down,		wankende beidiu an und abe,
pitching hither and thither.		ündende hin unde her.
so *drifts* the aimless desire,		sus swebet diu wiselose ger,
the mind uncertain of love,		der ungewisse minnen muot,
just as the ship without anchor does	*ship without anchor*	reht als daz schif ane anker tuot
in like manner.		in ebengelicher wise.
The charming Isolde, the wise,		die gevüege Isot, diu wise,
the young, sweet queen,		diu junge süeze künigin
so drew she thoughts in	*drew* *thoughts, in*	also zoch si gedanken in
out of many hearts' sanctums	*hearts*	uz maneges herzen arken,
as the lodestone does the ships	*lodestone* *ships*	als der agestein die barken
with the Sirens' song.	*Sirens*	mit der Syrenen sangetuot.

In this passage, Gottfried compares Isolde's ability to attract hearts and thoughts with the classical story of the Sirens who attracted the mariners' attention by their song. The ships were then drawn to the rocks by the lodestone or magnet mountain. This comparison is suggested in the first nine lines and reiterated in the last six.[5] In the central twelve lines, Gottfried takes the equation "Isolde draws hearts = Sirens draw ships," extracts one part of it, namely hearts = ships, and develops it independently. The comparison is developed in the first eight lines of the central twelve and pointed in the final four lines. This expanded simile is actually presented in the form of an interpolation, a generalization developed out of a specific situation—a technique frequently used by Gottfried.

The division between the outer and inner groups is stressed by the fact that the word-play in the outer lines is restricted to these parts and is not repeated in the inner group of lines. The link between the two parts is fashioned primarily by the rhyme which runs over: *ungemache : sache, wise : wise.* The words *Siren, lodestone, ships, drew, hearts, thoughts, in* from the first part are repeated in almost exactly reverse order in the third part. The minor variations—*ziehent* is not repeated except as *zoch,* and the word for ship is varied—and the slight change in order prevent the unfortunate impression that would be made if the words appeared exactly reversed.

If the arc of the surrounding outer groups tends to direct attention to the inner group, the inner group of lines may be said to be constructed on the same principle. Although it falls into groups of eight and four lines, the word repetitions and the enclosing *uo* rhymes—*muot : guot, muot : tuot*—are restricted to the periphery. The theme itself—the fickleness or instability of the human spirit—is concentrated in the central lines. This lack of stability is strikingly expressed by the use of contradictory associations: *steady course* (at sea) and *uncertain haven* or harbor. This contradiction is, then, pictorially expressed in the concentration of words for "unanchored"—*tossing, pitching, up and down, hither and thither.* This picture is carried over into the summation of the simile with the words *drifts* and *aimless* and immediately ushers in the repetition of the key words by transferring the *uncertain* from the *harbor* to the *mind.* This conclusion, beginning with *so . . . ,* contrasts with the earlier

seldom and *often;* and beginning and end are further linked by
the repetition not only of the phrase *ship without anchor* but also
of the word *mind* and the words *comparison* and *like manner*
(*zebenmazene* and *in ebengelicher*).

Such a detailed set of verbal relationships—and not all have
been discussed—is very common in Gottfried's work and is
one of the most characteristic elements of his style. However,
it should not be inferred that such passages are pieces of
virtuosity unrelated to the context. The word *sange* in the last
line, an important aspect of the Siren simile, has as yet been un-
developed, although it actually provided the basis for the introduction of the simile. Gottfried now picks up this word and
develops it in the following passage. He begins, this time, with
a statement concerning Isolde: "She sang openly and secretly,
in through ears and eyes to where many a heart was stirred"
(8112–14; p. 148). The following explanation and amplification
of this connecting statement, together with the conclusion, in
which her talents are summarized, occupies, like the passage
just discussed, twenty-seven lines. On the other hand, enough has
been said about the importance of the voyage motif—one has
only to think of the "haven" in which the love potion is drunk—
for it to be evident that this simile has far-reaching connotations.

The analysis of a single short passage provides sufficient
evidence of the complex and detailed organization which char-
acterizes Gottfried's style. The principle which underlies the
relationship of key words in this excerpt is basic throughout
the work. Beginning and end are linked and point inward, as
it were, toward the center, while certain of the elements are
also related to earlier or later passages. Over and over again,
Gottfried employs this principle, the complexity of the inter-
relationships of the key words being usually a measure of the
importance of the individual passage within the context of the
work as a whole.

This principle is, however, not only used to deepen and en-
hance the meaning of an individual passage or to relate separated
scenes and episodes. It is, in fact, the extension of a principle
which can be employed in a single line, for example "*ein man ein
wip, ein wip ein man*" (129; p. 43). Here, too, the direction
is inward, toward the unexpressed synthesis of complementary
elements. In the passage quoted above, Gottfried had counter-

balanced identical words which directed attention toward the center, where he had united contradictory elements; on the one hand, the steadiness (security/constancy) of the sea journey and on the other the lack of security in the harbor. Antitheses of this nature form the principle *in nuce* of Gottfried's style; it is the expression, in the most concise form, of the bilateral symmetry referred to above, which may be contained in one line—*"ein man ein wip, ein wip ein man"* or in a quatrain:

> Their life, their death are our bread.
> Thus lives their life, thus lives their death.
> Thus they live and are yet dead
> And their death is the bread of the living. (237–40; p. 44)

It may also be extended over a lengthy passage. The underlying principle is always the same: the *coniunctio oppositorum*, the embracing of possibly disparate but inseparable factors within a unity which suggests a synthesis at a higher level.

III *Irony and Humor*

Closely related to the principle of the union of opposites is the other dominant feature of Gottfried's style, namely irony. If the inexpressible can find its expression through the consensus of opposites, that is, the impossible can be sought in the fusion of irreconcilable elements, what is not apparent may also be made evident by stressing the appearance, and the truth may be revealed by emphasizing the false unreality. The fundamental method of irony is the expression of the opposite of that which is to be understood, and this makes it at once a most valuable device, but also the most elusive of stylistic elements. The extensive use of irony by Gottfried is probably the greatest single factor contributing to the lack of agreement as to the meaning of his poem, and one which engenders, even today, opposite interpretations of one and the same passage. An example of this is the ordeal in which generations of scholars saw Gottfried's "criticism" as blasphemy; even today this view is not entirely without support. Generally, however, it is now accepted that Gottfried's comments on this episode are, on the contrary, an ironic commentary on those who—like Mark and his barons—view God in such a primitive and essentially blasphemous manner by imputing human qualities to Him.

Although the degree and function of irony varies throughout the work, there is a consistency in its use. It is not employed in the digressions; it is most frequently the basic element in the humor; and in narrative passages it is most difficult to pinpoint. In the digressions, Gottfried's earnestness of purpose, his evident desire to instruct and preach, leads to a directness of expression which is the very opposite of irony. Presumably he was as well aware as anyone that irony is easily overlooked and consequently —while enjoying the thought that it might be overlooked in the narrative by those at whom it was directed—was not willing to run the risk of failing to drive home the lesson for those for whom he was primarily writing.

The earnestness of the digressions is matched, however, by the spontaneity of the humor; and it is in such humorous inter-polations that we can most easily grasp Gottfried's use of irony. At the end of the Gandin episode, for example, he says of the lovers as they return to court: "Whether they attained happiness anywhere on the way, resting among the flowers, I shall leave unguessed; for my part I shall refrain from guesses and surmises" (13,432–37; p. 218). And even at such serious moments as that in the final orchard scene, as the lovers are about to be surprised by Mark, Gottfried's humor breaks through: "Tristan and Isolde were both sleeping after I know not what kind of exertion" (18,212–14; p. 280). In both cases, the irony is self-evident and couched in its classical simple form of *ironeia*—the feigned ignorance of truth. Gottfried knows the truth full well, and the reader is hardly likely to miss the point; but when Gottfried describes the beauty of Isolde as Mark looks down on her sleeping in the grotto and says: "Heaven knows of what exertion the tale tells that might have flushed her cheeks" (17,561–63; p. 272), the irony—if irony it is—is less obvious, for Gottfried adds after a few lines: "Yes, I recall what her exertions were. Isolde, as I said just now, had sauntered through the dew to the meadow that morning, and this is what had given her her color" (17,570–75; p. 272). Is this a genuine explanation or double irony? In this case, we view it as irony, since the two remarks are separated by lines emphasizing the sensual im-pression of Isolde's beauty, and because the whole passage seems subsequently to be recalled by Gottfried in the lines quoted above from the orchard scene. The example serves, however, to demonstrate how fine the distinction is.

The importance of the element of irony in Gottfried's work cannot be overestimated, for on it rests, in large measure, the correct understanding of many of the episodes—for example of the ordeal referred to above. Whereas the non-blasphemous nature of Gottfried's remarks in that episode is now generally accepted, it is far from clear whether the portrayal of such characters as Rivalin and the exploits of Tristan are to be taken at face value or as ironic. Do they represent an adherence to accepted values or a subtle denigration of the cherished but superficial view of the meaning of chivalry? We have already suggested in our interpretation that Gottfried's portrayal is in essence ironic, that by overemphasis of the often quoted tenets of chivalry and by contrasting the failure of those who follow the rules with the success of Tristan, who ignores them, he depicts the futility of these exercises. We referred, at that time, to Rivalin, and we now again use his career as an example.

Portrayed, at first, as an exceptionally noble and valiant youth, whose rashness should be excused by his very youthfulness, Rivalin appears at Mark's court as a model knight. His praises are sung by the ladies in hyperbolic fashion, but his reputation and the impression made on these ladies compare curiously with his behavior in the passage immediately following, when he is shown as helplessly confused by Blancheflor's not over-subtle remark. When he finally realizes its significance and responds, it is still she who holds the initiative. From now on, he does all the right things but with entirely wrong results. Finally he is killed in the battle with Morgan, and his wife and whole kingdom are left desolate. In praising Rivalin, the ladies at Mark's court had said: "What a *blissful* man! The woman that wins him will be *fortunate* indeed" (716–18; p. 51). When Gottfried describes the death of Rivalin and its effect on his followers who were "all equally dead since they lost everything which gives men *bliss* and a *fortunate* life" (1698–702; p. 63), surely this repetition of the key words points to the irony of Rivalin's life, so perfectly chivalrous and yet so utterly futile.

A similar, but rather less pointed, use of irony is provided by the description of the battle with Urgan (15,915–16,212; pp. 250–54). In this case, Tristan is introduced as being by reputation a most "manly man." He cuts a poor figure in the battle, however, although he does succeed in defeating Urgan after first having cut off his hand. The "happily victorious" Tristan then picks up "his [Tristan's!] hand" and goes back to Gilan bearing this trophy—"the dead hand of the giant." The passage ends with a repetition of the phrase "a manly man," followed immediately by a second use of the phrase "Tristan the happily victorious."

Taken out of context and stressed in this fashion, such phrases may well seem ironic in intent; but it must not be forgotten that they are widely separated and used without special emphasis other than that which accrues to them from their position at the beginning and the end of the narrative passage. But it is only on such slender evidence that the assessment of whether or not irony is intended can be based. These echoing phrases must give us pause and make us reflect that there is perhaps, after all, a certain discrepancy between the word and the deed, between theory and practice. What is repeated—"for Brutus is an honorable man"—tends to become suspect.

There is frequent use of irony in Gottfried's work, and we contend that it is characteristic of the poet's attitude. But it is not the irony of a man who has doubts about the validity of everything; it is not the ironic detachment of one who sees through everything without having himself a position from which to judge. Gottfried knows where he stands, and the very earnestness of his purpose and his consequent restraint from irony at those points where he is especially anxious not to be misunderstood prevent any such assumption. It is evident, in fact, that his primary intent is the establishment of his positive view, and that the deflation of contemporary attitudes is a secondary purpose. In addition, his tendency toward ironic detachment from the subject leads in the direction of humor rather than of cynicism or satire, suggesting that despite all his seriousness he is eminently aware of the absurdity of exaggeration and one-sideness, and appreciative of the necessity of maintaining a sense of proportion. It is for this reason that we have quoted examples of ironic humor from the most serious scene. This humor is also a very significant, though often overlooked, element in a work which is normally noted for its learned and polemic qualities, and we shall therefore refer in some detail to the nature of the humor and the humorous intent.

There are brief flashes of humor and humorous interludes everywhere throughout the work, even, as we have seen, in the most serious scenes. No one, not even Tristan, escapes this barb, and in the Urgan scene, for example, he is the object of the ironic humor of the giant who, having cut Tristan's horse in half, begs Tristan to deign to dismount. But no scenes are more delightful in their humor than those which involve the Steward at the Irish court, the would-be lover of Isolde. He first appears on the scene in full flight, as Tristan goes out to seek the dragon. He always went out when the others did, says Gottfried, but only to be seen with them. He never saw the dragon without valorously turning tail.

When this Steward, who has surmised from the dragon's death roar that the beast must have expired, returns to the scene, he first comes upon Tristan's charred and half-eaten horse, at which point he again wavers for some time before overcoming his fears. Following the dragon's trail, he comes upon the beast's body so unexpectedly that he almost falls off his horse. Having gathered his wits, he turns the horse, but so violently that they both fall to the ground in a heap. At this stage, he cannot even delay to remount but runs away on foot. Certain that the dragon has not pursued him, he stealthily returns, recovers his spear and remounts, moving off to a safe distance to view the body. Convinced, finally, that the dragon really is harmless, he charges it bravely with his spear, uttering encouraging battle cries. His wits are still, however, very much about him, for he breaks off the "fight" to look for the real victor, with the villainous intent, of course, of murdering him if necessary—weakened, as he would be, from his struggle with the dragon. When he finds no one, he resumes the battle at close quarters—with his sword—before returning to the city to spread the news of his exploit.

Before the court, the Steward boasts in a ludicrous fashion but also shows himself to have understanding. His retort to Isolde, when she flatly refuses to have any truck with him, contains a strong element of truth, namely that women are enamored of contradictions. Their contrariness leads them to love the one who hates them and reject the one who loves them, an oblique commentary on the problem which does later face Isolde. The Queen mother, however, neatly disposes of this argument by pointing out to the Steward that he is guilty of doing the same thing and is, therefore, behaving in a womanish way, when he claims to be such a man. The actual confrontation of the Steward with the real slayer of the dragon is prepared in great detail and, of course, largely for the sake of Tristan and Isolde. A certain element of dramatic irony is present, for the Steward seems not to believe in the existence of any such competitor, although the reader knows it full well, and the Queen deliberately encourages him in this belief by hesitating to produce her champion. Ultimately, the Steward puts himself into such an impossible position that his friends must dissuade him from what would inevitably have been an ignominious defeat at the hands of Tristan.

The humor varies in this episode from the sheer ludicrous, almost slapstick, comedy of the Steward's "battle" with the dragon to the satirical interchange between him and the two Isoldes before the court. But all this takes place concurrently with the action around Tristan, his discovery, healing, and unmasking; and while there is a strong element of contrast between these parallel actions, there is, nevertheless, no lack of humor in those scenes involving Tristan. The absurdity of his situation, for example, as he sits in the bath while the two Isoldes lament over his treachery and consider whether or not he should be killed, is admirably pointed by Brangane, who says, when asked for her view: "Think it over yourself. But let us withdraw and let him leave the bath" (10,406–7; p. 178). Later, when Tristan throws himself at their feet, they all look away and at each other—"and so they stood, and so he lay. 'My Lady,' said Brangane, 'the knight has lain there too long'" (10,478–79; p. 179). Humorous, too, is the younger Isolde's explanation of how she discovered the secret of the names Tantris/Tristan. At great length she unfolds this to her mother—treated elsewhere as a wise woman, versed in all manner of arts including divination!— who is so impressed that she crosses herself in wonderment. And, of course, the entire action takes place against the background of the alternate fear and concern, rage and jealousy on the part of the barons, who had accompanied him on the voyage and who are now anxiously cooped up in the ship while Tristan is basking in the warm solicitude of the three women.

If we have dwelt on the question of humor at some length, it is not because we feel that it is an especially important aspect of the work, but rather because it is an aspect often passed over in the pursuit of deeper meaning. The humor infuses the whole work and is as important and valid a characteristic as any other toward the full understanding of the poem. It is one of the *major* elements in Gottfried's style, along with his sense of irony, structure, and proportion. Gottfried is a great artist and preserves in all things his sense of balance, in mood as much as in structure or in human understanding; and this style of his contributes substantially to an understanding of his work, in that it contributes to our knowledge of the poet. If "manners makyth man," then it might be said that the manner of writing, the style, *is* the poet.

IV *Summary*

If we were asked for one word or phrase which would sum up the essential quality of Gottfried's style, we would choose the simple word *both*. In *Tristan* this word occurs approximately three hundred and fifty times in 19,500 lines as compared with only one hundred and sixty-five instances in the *Nibelungenlied*—which is of the same length—and only two hundred and fifty in Wolfram's *Parzival*, which is considerably longer (25,000 lines). These are of course only hollow statistics, but they do indicate the relative frequency of a word which Gottfried employs in a variety of ways. Such a word count is also valuable since the German forms *beide, beider* and so forth are often avoided in English translation, where *both* is either replaced by two or dropped from the text. For example, in the relatively insignificant passage in which the behavior of Rual and Floraete is described after the death of Blancheflor, the word *beid–* occurs four times in the German. In Hatto's translation the word *both* appears only once; in the other instances it is simply omitted where it is used in the original with the personal pronoun.

The word *both* is used by Gottfried chiefly in two forms: either in the form *both* this *and* that or in apposition to the personal pronoun, *both* of them, *both* of us and so forth. In the first case, the use of *both . . . and* not only emphasizes the things included but stresses also the unexpectedness, so to speak, of their association. This is, essentially, the use also in English. Modern German, however, no longer uses this form in standard language. As might be expected, Gottfried uses *both* in this way to link together opposites, as for example, in lines 1295–96: "Both from love and also from sorrow her body's strength was sapped away." In the second case, *both* is used to stress the unity and oneness of the persons—or things—referred to. This use is extremely common, *both* of them, *both* of us and similar forms occurring, for example, twenty-three times in the course of the eavesdropping scene (14,302–906). The most impressive use of the word occurs in lines 14,330–32: "the evil of both, the good of both, the death of both, the life of both, they were woven together as in one" (p. 230).

It is noteworthy that in the passage just quoted the word *one* occurs also in a stressed position. On numerous occasions, Gottfried increases the force of the word *both* by juxtaposing the word *one* with it. This was also done in the passage quoted above concerning Rual and Floraete. They were, says Gottfried, "to God and the world both one loyalty and one body" (1802–3; p. 65). Of Rivalin and Blancheflor he had earlier said: "In their mind both had one love and one desire" (1356–57; p. 58). In such cases, the *both* is to be associated not only with the two persons, who are as one, but also with the two objects. These belong together but are stressed as being singular, since the two persons are only one.

Gottfried's use of the simple word *both* is a succinct expression of his style and typical of his thought. Whilst the phrase *both* this *and* (also) that may link naturally related or complementary elements, it is employed by Gottfried mainly to unite polarities or disparate elements. For polarities *must* be united to be fulfilled; the obverse and the reverse must *both* be accepted. There is nothing which does not have its opposite, and it is the opposite which gives it meaning. It is this belief in the significance of the *coniunctio oppositorum* which infuses Gottfried's style at every level from the bilateral symmetry of the structural elements through irony and humor to the chiasmus and oxymoron of individual lines and phrases. It is his philosophy *in nuce*.

CHAPTER 5

Modern Literary Versions and Scholarly Interpretations of Tristan

LITERATURE is a continuing process, and while each work is an expression of the author's contemporary situation, each author nevertheless builds upon his predecessors. Gottfried's *Tristan* may be, from the absolute esthetic standpoint, the greatest achievement in the long history of the Tristan theme, but it is at the same time, only a part of this development. His achievement did not cause the development to cease; on the contrary it provided the point of departure for future versions, especially in the modern period. In order to explain what this story has come to mean to us today, it is, therefore, necessary to say something both about these modern literary versions and about the modern understanding, that is, scholarly interpretation, of Gottfried's work.

By modern versions we mean primarily those literary embodiments of the Tristan story subsequent to the rediscovery by scholars in the late eighteenth and early nineteenth century of the literary works of the medieval period. The aim of the poet is to present the theme as he understands it and as he feels it relates to his contemporary audience. The aim of the scholar, on the other hand, is usually understood to be the establishment, as far as is possible, of the full meaning of the work in its *own* time. It is true that the poet may be influenced by scholarly interpretations of his source material, but the two functions of poet and scholar should not be confused. In the nineteenth century, unfortunately, and to a lesser degree also in the early twentieth, scholars took it upon themselves to analyze modern versions of the Tristan theme on the basis of their knowledge of the source material and to judge them more or less according to their fidelity to the source, rather than by their merits or shortcomings as literary works.[1]

Our concern in the following discussion is not to establish the degree of faithfulness to the original, but neither is it to condemn or praise such modern versions on the basis of preconceived, absolute literary-esthetic criteria. Our only interest is to judge the extent to which the Tristan theme—largely represented by Gottfried von Strassburg—has inspired poets to attempt literary versions which express contemporary understanding of the elemental human situation which this story contains. In so doing, we must naturally be selective, since the number of versions is very large, and we shall naturally select those that we consider most successful or representative.[2]

I *From the Middle Ages to Romanticism*

Before discussing nineteenth- and twentieth-century reworkings of the story, it is necessary to survey briefly the later medieval and Renaissance versions of the legend, which usually constitute, together with the older works, the major source of the modern versions. Only after the Renaissance did the story largely disappear from view; and when it was rediscovered little distinction was made between the various forms which it had taken during the later Middle Ages and the Renaissance. The prose translation of Thomas' poem which had been made by Brother Robert for King Haakon of Norway became the major source for northern versions, for the Icelandic saga of around 1400, the shorter song—*Tristrams kvaedi*—of the end of the fifteenth century and the folk tales.[3] The same version by Thomas was also the source for the Middle English *Sir Tristrem*,[4] a lengthy stanzaic poem composed toward the end of the thirteenth century. In the sole surviving manuscript, this work contains three hundred and four eleven-line stanzas. The conclusion is lacking, but an attempt to supply the missing stanzas in the original language and form was made by Sir Walter Scott.[5]

A later French version—from the mid-thirteenth century on in various forms—usually known as the prose romance, is a typical example of the late medieval treatment of courtly literature.[6] Material from numerous and diversified sources was knitted together, expanded, repeated in variant forms, and lengthened in every conceivable way. In this manner, the *Tristan* became an enormously lengthy work of perhaps a thousand pages or more, in which not only the innumerable exploits of Tristan himself but also generations of his ancestors are described. The Tristan story is here related also to the Arthurian cycle, and the original simplicity is lost beneath a mass of detailed and repetitious action. The emphasis in all of these works is essentially on action rather than contemplation, on description rather than thought.

This French prose work[7] was the source for other Romance versions—Spanish and Italian—and even for a Russian version. In England, Sir Thomas Malory completed in 1469 his *Morte d'Arthur*, a lengthy compilation of Arthurian material from French sources, and included in it the Tristan story.[8] His work became a basic source of material for modern versions of Arthurian legends and of the Tristan legend in English literature. Malory's position in the development of the Tristan theme is an interesting one. On the threshold of the modern period—his work was one of the first books to appear in print—he looks back to the Golden Age of chivalry and endeavors, through his description of it, to reawaken in his readers something of the philosophy of that period. His treatment of the French source is not uncritical and may be summed up as an attempt to reduce the incoherent mass of Arthurian material to a simpler and better organized whole and to depict in more distinct form the positive features of the chivalric ethic.

The manuscript which Malory probably used for the Tristan portion of his narrative has been reduced very greatly, possibly to 15 to 20 per cent of its original length,[9] but the picture which is given of Tristan is hardly altered, presumably because it well suited the author's purpose. In the French prose romance, Tristan had become one of the noblest of Arthur's knights, involved in an interminable number of chivalrous exploits. He is the knightly hero par excellence who never betrays his calling or his love, and it is noteworthy that the French romance ends with Tristan's dying words to Segremor in which he says adieu to "the *chivalry* I have loved and honored" and kisses his sword![10] His unimpeachable loyalty is contrasted by Malory with the ignoble and treacherous behavior of Mark, and Tristan therefore owes no loyalty to Mark, but only to Isolde. The death of the lovers is not described by Malory, but it is stated that Tristan was later murdered by Mark in Isolde's presence: "Shamefully that false traitor King Mark slew him as he sat harping afore his lady La Beale Isoud" (II, 348–49).

The same tendencies which produced the prose romance in France resulted in a quite different version of the Tristan romance in Germany. Even Gottfried's version had been completed shortly after his death on the basis of Eilhart rather than Thomas; and when the romance was turned into prose during the fifteenth century,[11] it was again to Eilhart that the unknown author turned. This chapbook version appeared in Augsburg in 1484— Malory's appeared in 1485—and a later edition at Worms in 1549/50 became the source for Hans Sachs. The chapbook simplifies the story greatly, putting it into prose "on account of those people who do not like such rhymed books" (p. 202), but it maintains—despite the presence of Arthur and his knights—the original form of the plot. The beginning has been considerably reduced: the marriage of Rivalin and Blancheflor is consented to by Mark; although Blancheflor dies in childbirth, Rivalin remains alive; Tristan comes voluntarily to Cornwall, where his being knighted is passed over in one line; so that the way is open after the minimum of delay for the main episode, the battle with Morold. The remainder of the work follows the usual outline and need not be discussed. Instead, we shall look at the manner in which the love potion and the resulting relationship are portrayed.

When the princess Isolde is about to leave Ireland, her mother prepares the love potion, of which the author, even before its intent or malfunction is mentioned, says: "It might well be called the accursed potion" (p. 42). After describing the intended effect, he continues: "When, however, the four years were past, then one of them might leave the other despite the drink" (p. 43). Since this temporary efficacy of the potion is at variance with the story—Tristan's love still torments him after his banishment—the author hastens to add that after such a long period of great love it was not possible for the flame of love to die out, "and they therefore had to burn in the flame of great and unspeakably strong love all their life" (p. 44). The immediate effects of the potion are later given in some detail. The symptoms of love are enumerated and Isolde breaks into a long and impassioned monologue. Tristan's emotions are not analyzed to the same extent; and the author contents himself with the statement that his complaints were twice as great, "for men knew always much prettier and more expressive words than women" (p. 49).

In this scene, and throughout the remainder of the work, the love of Tristan and Isolde is entirely motivated by the effect of the "accursed drink" and the sinful relationship thus excused by external compulsion. As soon as the effect of the potion has worn off, they return to the hermit who had previously refused Tristan absolution and confess their sin. Their immediate decision is, in other words, to return to "normal" life, although their love is supposed so to have taken root as to be henceforth ineradicable. Although the King banishes Tristan, despite the latter's protestations of willingness to make amends, he later declares, when he is told the true facts, that he would willingly have renounced his kingdom and spent his days in poverty had he known the truth.

This last passage, in which Mark discovers the truth and the author then offers his moral, exposes the basic ambivalence of attitude within the chapbook version. The love relationship is viewed as sinful and excused only by the potion; yet Mark would have allowed the lovers their will, had he known the truth, and the "sinful" love of Tristan and Isolde is contrasted with contemporary lack of understanding of true love. The author describes, for example, the hardships which Tristan and Isolde bear during two years in the forest and states that a couple would, in his time, not be willing to undergo even two months of such a life (cf. Gottfried, ll. 12,187ff.).

Tristan's opponents are depicted as representative of the evil qualities in man. In particular, Auctrat and the dwarf are severely condemned, Auctrat being described as a cousin of Tristan and therefore doubly treacherous, and the dwarf as a tool of Satan, an "accursed creature, hateful and unpleasing to God and the world" (p. 80). He therefore sympathizes with Tristan as with an honest man beset by treacherous villains and poltroons, and not a word of criticism falls during the narration of Tristan's exploits after his banishment, that is, of his clandestine visits to Isolde. Despite all this, however, the author introduces his moral at the very end: "Take heed yourselves, that worldly love does not overcome you, that you thereby forget the love of God and come to such an untimely end. Take note how love brought these two to such an early and unprepared death" (pp. 201–202).

This same attitude can be even more clearly seen in the work of Hans Sachs (1494–1576), whose protestant bourgeois soul led him to cap every story with a moral, no matter how unrelated it might be to the text. He treated the Tristan material in two very different forms, in a group of "Master-songs" *(Meisterlieder)* and in a full-length drama.[12] In both cases, the nature of the *genre* demands great selection and compression, but Sachs has instinctively seized on the main elements of the action. Of particular interest in this connection is the order of composition of the *Meisterlieder*. He began with the potion scene and the following adventures (December 4, 1551) and took the plot through the discovery of the lovers and their flight to the forest in the second song (December 5, 1551). The next two songs in chronological order treat the episodes preceding the potion scene—the battle with Morold and with the dragon (both on December 7, 1551)—and in the fifth song he turns to the period after the lovers have been separated, selecting the most popular episode of Tristan in the disguise of a jester (December 11, 1551). Not until fifteen months later, after completing his drama, did Sachs finally conclude the story with a song on the death of Tristan (March 13, 1553).

The action of the *Tragedia* is also reduced to the bare essentials, the only notable difference being perhaps the omission of any reference to Brangane's substitution for Isolde on the wedding night. This and similar episodes are either passed over in silence or else narrated by the "herald." For example, Tristan's journey to Ireland to obtain a cure for his wound does not form part of the action. After his departure the herald reports: "People say that Tristan has gone unrecognized to Ireland. . . . There he is said to have found a female doctor to heal his wound. The King has word that he will return shortly hale and hearty" (p. 149). Almost all other action is reported in this manner with the result that the whole work has a recitative rather than dramatic character.

One must assume from Sachs' handling of the material that he was not anxious to show any approval of the love relationship, since he takes every opportunity to reduce the impact of this theme by cutting characteristic features which even the chapbook contains. For example, the scene in which Tristan and Isolde drink the potion is reduced to twelve lines in which each says he or she is moved by a strange emotion. There is no monologue, no confession of love, and no subsequent meeting. Although Curvenal and Brangane agree to permit such a meeting, the following scene already shows their arrival in Cornwall.

Although Brangane has stated that the potion will make them love for four years, there is no suggestion that they must continue to love at the end of the period, nor indeed any reference to the cessation of the potion's effect when the time has elapsed. When they are discovered in the forest by the King, Isolde advises that they go to the hermit, confess their sin, and request his intercession with Mark, "since we have lived here now in sorrow and suffering for two years. Now you see: there is no chance of continuing with this life, Tristan. The King knows that we are here in this part of the wilderness" (p. 173). The motivation—insofar as there is any—would appear to be the pointlessness of their life in view of their discovery by the King.

Neither here nor in the following scenes is the continuation of Tristan's love explained, but merely assumed. The only direct reference to the love relationship is, therefore, contained in the concluding speech of the herald, where the substance of the chapbook moral is justified and expanded upon, until it becomes the longest single speech in the entire work (38 lines, pp. 184–85). After showing how "such irregular love" drives both young and old into wicked ways and a sorrowful state, the herald—after citing Diogenes and Petrarch—passes to the way in which those who love suffer from "over-anxiety, longing, separation, parting, gossip, and secret envy." The end is inevitably "the loss of God's grace." His final statement is: "Be warned, then, by this, oh Man, against the snares of such love and spare your love until marriage; then have but one love and no more." Further comment on the author's intent or on the gap which separates him from Gottfried is hardly necessary.

In Gottfried's time, this romance, like its Arthurian counterparts, had been infused with an ideal to which the material was subservient. In the later, bourgeois period, the story alone constitutes the sole interest and, therefore, also the sole content; and no other than the superficial meaning could and would be derived from it. The moral which is put forward—death is the reward of sin and the punishment for sinful love—is, therefore, at variance with the original intent of the story and even with the writer's feelings. The chapbook version, nevertheless, remained popular throughout the fifteenth and sixteenth centuries and was included in the collection known as the *Book of Love,* last printed in 1587.[13] After this, the romance disappears from view, although references to the figures of Tristan and Isolde— for example in Andreas Gryphius' *Horribilicribrifax*[14]—prove that it was not forgotten. It was almost two hundred years before the romance appeared in print again, but once discovered, there followed an endless succession of editions, translations, adaptations, and commentaries.

II *From the Romantics to Wagner*

The revival of interest in the Tristan theme was one aspect of a general revival of interest in the Middle Ages and the Renaissance which is often attributed to the Romantics. It is true that even today popular conceptions of medieval life are still conditioned by Romantic portrayals of the period, which are often highly "romanticized," since the Romantics derived their material from late medieval or Renaissance, rather than from original, sources. On the other hand, it must not be forgotten that the Romantics—except for those few who had access to the manuscripts—could only use these works after they had been published. Romantic interest in the past is, in fact, preceded by historical and antiquarian, that is, by scholarly, interest in the period, which led to the unearthing and publication of literary works.

Earlier critics, such as J. J. Bodmer (1698–1783), had taken steps in this direction, and at the beginning of the Romantic era the work of publication was carried on by scholars such as C. H. Myller (1740–1807) and J. G. Büsching (1783–1829). As early as 1776, the Tristan romance had been published in an adaptation from the French prose romance by Count Tressan in the *Bibliothèque universelle des romans,*[15] but this version, though known in Germany and reprinted more than once before the end of the century, appears to have had no great influence either on scholars or on poets. It was only with the publication of an edition of Gottfried's *Tristan* that genuine interest was aroused. The first edition of Gottfried was produced by C. H.

Myller in 1785 in the second part of his *Collection of German Poems from the Twelfth, Thirteenth and Fourteenth Century*.[16] A more scholarly edition was produced by Groote in 1821.[17] In addition, the *Book of Love* was republished in 1809 by von der Hagen and Büsching.[18]

The interest of the German Romantics in the literature of the Middle Ages was not solely due to a feeling of having discovered a kindred poetic world. They did, of course, feel this affinity, for as A. W. Schlegel put it: "Later [romantic poetry] is indeed not romantic just because it is modern, but rather because it concurs with the sentiments of the chivalric age and is an echo of those magnificent natural sounds."[19] But an element of pragmatism is undoubtedly present in much of the discussion of the Middle Ages. Medieval literature, which evidently includes the period through the sixteenth century, is used as a stick with which to beat those who turn to the classical literature of antiquity or the classicist literature of France for their models; and the originality of medieval works is contrasted with the lack of originality in contemporary literature.

Furthermore, there is an evident desire to instil a sense of pride in past German achievements—"chivalry was a German invention"[20]—despite the fact that A. W. Schlegel lays great emphasis on the supranational character of medieval literature. There is, therefore, in German Romanticism—unlike English Romanticism—a strongly didactic strain, a combination of theory, teaching, and practice, which, while it may have furthered knowledge of the Tristan romance and medieval literature in general, did not lead to any adequate interpretation of the poem or any successful literary adaptation of the theme. It is, nevertheless, of interest to look at these attempts, for both the critical judgments and the literary versions in the period up to the 1820's set the pattern for succeeding generations.

Perhaps most characteristic of the period is A. W. Schlegel, who discusses Gottfried's *Tristan* briefly in the course of his lectures on "Romantic Poetry" delivered in Berlin in the years 1803–4 and who mentions his own attempt to put this romance into German verse. Although he had planned to compose a vast epic, which would include not only the *Tristan* but also the whole of the Arthurian material including the grail legend, he never progressed beyond the first ninety-one stanzas. These were published as a fragment in 1811.[21] In these stanzas, Tristan's early life up to his abduction by the Norwegian merchants is recounted; and with minor deviations the text is faithful to Gottfried.

The only other significant version of the Tristan story[22] at this time is a short outline by Platen for a drama on the subject, but this outline—made in the years 1825–28—was never developed.[23] Only the first scene of the first act and a song intended for the end of Act II were written. The plot centers around the enmity of Tristan and his cousin Auctrat, rather than around the love of Tristan and Isolde. The action begins at the wedding of Isolde and Mark, when Auctrat betrays Tristan, who is banished. Unappeased, Auctrat follows Tristan and wounds him with a poisoned arrow. It is again Auctrat who tells Tristan of the supposed black sail, thereby bringing about his death. When Isolde arrives, she kills herself.

The Romantics failed to produce any complete or even promising version of *Tristan;* and the question arises: Why did this romance, which seems to us to be as if made for "Romantic" treatment, fail to inspire a Romantic re-creation?

Without a lengthy discussion of Romantic philosophy and literature such a question is not fully answerable; but it would seem that the root of the problem lies in the nature of the material and the contemporary understanding of it. Stripped of all details, the story is one that lauds adulterous love and extols the means whereby it is enjoyed, at the same time as condemning the wronged husband. The idea of the soul mate and the precedence of true love over marriage might well have been acceptable to the Romantics, but the love of Tristan and Isolde is a worldly love, based on a desire for *life*. Even the invocations of the deity, culminating in the blasphemous oath, are all directed toward this one end—to prolong life and the present enjoyment of love. Gottfried's lovers neither seek nor long for death but, on the contrary, avoid it. To the Romantics, the essence of love lies in its spiritual, transcendental quality. The meaning of the love experience is the ability to transcend the limitations of the world of physical experience, to partake of the universal nature of love, to be one with the beloved and with the world soul. Ultimately this leads to the longing for release from the limitations of the world and the flesh and for union with this world soul, which can only be achieved through death.

The attitude of such critics as A. W. Schlegel and of the poets of the Romantic period is, therefore, one of a desire to accept *Tristan* but inability to approve of it without reservation. Schlegel, for example, links it with *Lancelot* in contrast to *Parzival,* saying: "From the deeds of a Parzivall or Tyturell which are directed toward holy and mystical ends, to the lascivious, forbidden, and yet to a certain degree innocent, love affairs of Lancelot or Tristan. . . ."[24] In his review of the 1809 edition of the *Book of Love,* Jakob Grimm also discusses Gottfried, comparing his work unfavorably with the chapbook: "Gottfried's poem is one of the most delightful poems in the world; it is like a mirror of charm and heartfelt love, but not without something disturbing and a certain artificial lack of coherence."[25]

Approximately at the same time as the reissue of the *Book of Love,* there appeared the first scholarly study of Gottfried, which gave (almost) outright approval to his work. This article by B. Docen[26] is by no means a profound study of *Tristan,* and it is typical for the time that he, too, is concerned with the moral of the work. This, in Docen's view, is the fact that an immoral escapade directly leads to Tristan's death. His approval of the poem as a whole, however, is couched in enthusiastic terms which were not to be repeated for many generations.

Much more typical, and certainly more influential, was the kind of judgment passed by the famous scholar Karl Lachmann in 1820. In a volume of selections from medieval poets he includes only a few excerpts from Gottfried, commenting: "Gottfried has only received his just deserts; his orderly, meaningfully embellished manner of narration is very evident from the passage chosen. The main parts of his effeminate and immoral story offer, however, nothing other than voluptuousness and blasphemy."[27] Such a comment is typical of the attitude toward *Tristan* displayed at this early period, although considerable attention was paid to the alleged historical, legendary, or mythological sources of the material.

In the decades immediately following the Romantic period, Lachmann's judgment was repeated in even more categorical and violent terms. In 1835[28] G. G. Gervinus praised Gottfried's artistry in reworking the material which in Eilhart is "so rude and distasteful" and "completely lacking in greatness and dignity" (p. 624); but he is, on the other hand, clearly concerned about the absence of any definite statement on the moral which, in his view, is inherent in the work. He regrets that we cannot tell whether the conclusion really would have shown us Tristan "as the plaything of fortune and passion, as the fruit and the sacrifice of the frivolity and peculiarity of the time" (p. 626). This is what Gervinus feels the work does show, even though Gottfried has not directly said so; and it is, therefore, not surprising that in his analysis of the plot Gervinus bluntly gives his own evaluation of the ethics of the action. What follows on the love potion "can arouse in us nothing but revulsion" (p. 629).

The poet Heinrich Laube[29] is less specific in his criticism, possibly from a realization that he has not properly understood the text. At all events, his discussion of the plot contains numerous errors of fact and may be passed over. In general, he views Gottfried as a counterpart to Wolfram, the latter representing the true, deeply serious nature of the Middle Ages, the former an almost frivolous nature, thus foreshadowing modern developments. In Gottfried, Laube sees the breakthrough of sensuality and a satiric attitude which makes him unique in his time, even a betrayer of his time, "the first betrayer and the greatest betrayer of the Middle Ages" (p. 108).

Given these views, it is certainly not surprising that A. Vilmar, a theologian, spoke in 1845[30] of "these stories of the Celts" in which "divine and human laws, divine and human rights are trampled upon . . . with a stubborn insolence and a naked shamelessness which . . . frequently fills one with distaste, even with revulsion." Gottfried, he says, "delights to go along with the world, even to guide it, to lust and enjoyment." In Wackernagel's *History of German Literature*[31] we are also told that Gottfried possesses "joy in a splendor that dazzles and deceives . . . besides this a distaste for all earnestness of purpose, a frivolity which has deprived the poem of any guiding thought, which . . . glosses over what is wrong and in order to do so does not recoil even from outrage against what is most sacred."

On the literary scene, however, the Tristan theme received rather better treatment. In 1839, Friedrich Rückert published a poetic fragment in the summer issue of G. O. Marbach's *Jahres-*

zeiten, in which the story of Tristan is picked up at the point where Schlegel had left off. It is carried on only briefly, and nothing further came of the venture. The fragment did have some consequences, however, in that it inspired the editor of the journal, Oswald Marbach, to attempt a translation of the first lines of Gottfried.[32] His version is certainly not free of errors, but it has some poetic merit and is, in any case, of interest as the first attempt at an accurate reproduction of the original, even to the extent of preserving, as far as possible, its metrical form. Any thought that Marbach might have had of carrying on with this work was frustrated by the appearance, in 1844, of a complete translation by Hermann Kurtz.[33]

To this same period also belongs the first extensive and partly successful reworking of *Tristan,* a verse "epic" by Karl Lebrecht Immermann. Immermann had planned his work as early as 1832 but made little progress until some years later, and when he died in 1840 it was still little more than half finished and was only published posthumously.[34] The first part, up to the arrival in Cornwall after the drinking of the love potion, is complete while the second part begins with the substitution of Brangane for Isolde and breaks off at the beginning of the episode in which Isolde plans Brangane's death. The remainder is available only in the form of a short prose outline.

Immermann varies considerably from his sources, but these changes do not to any extent affect the relationship between Tristan, Isolde, and Mark. Tristan's second journey to Ireland, for example, is eliminated, since Tristan, after being cured, is recognized as the slayer of Morold and saves himself by claiming to have been sent to ask the hand of Isolde for Mark. In essence, the outline remains the same: Tristan and Isolde drink the love potion on the journey to Cornwall; after various episodes their love is discovered; they are separated; Tristan marries Isolde Whitehand and sends for the first Isolde when he is dying. The same use is also made of the black and white sails.

In the depiction of the love of Tristan and Isolde there is, however, a significant departure. Previous to the drinking of the love potion, there is some indication that they could be in love; but the discovery of Tristan's true identity and his claim to be wooing her for Mark turn Isolde against him. On the ship, she is calmer than Tristan and renounces the prospect of love.

Tristan despairs at what he has done and, in his turn, decides to renounce the courtly life of pleasure in favor of service in the cause of Christianity. Danger and the prospect of death in fighting for the Holy Land seem to him the only fitting penance for his thoughtlessness, the only cure for his feelings. After the potion, all such thoughts vanish, for they were merely substitutions, ways of escape from the self and the truth. Tristan and Isolde now become one with each other and with nature.

At this point, the Romantic tendencies become very evident, and the detailed descriptions of nature, in particular of the sea, build to a climax which prepares the way for their later decision. Their union is natural, good, holy, even divinely ordained.[35] In each other they achieve that primordial unity which was lost by original sin and the symbol of which is the sea, which is divided by the ship but which closes behind it as it passes. The sea itself represents the boundlessness and depth of love and just as they see the soul through each other's eyes,[36] so shortly afterwards, they look into the depths of the ocean and feel one with it.

But the beauty of creation as they see it on the bed of the sea is built from just such dust as man is made of, and the desire to unite with this transient but imperishable nature makes itself felt: "Therefore, beloved, let us plunge our souls into the watery splendor and merge with that sweet symbol. Ah, if only we, too, were substance like that down there."[37] This is the romantic desire for union with nature and the universal soul; and it is not surprising that their first thought on being recalled to reality by the sight of Cornwall is suicide.[38] The suicide pact is prevented only by Brangane, who offers herself as a substitute for Isolde on the wedding night.

Thus far the motivation seems logical, but it is difficult to see how the results of this decision can be made acceptable in the latter part of the work, for soon all thought of death as preferable to separation or the shame of Isolde's being possessed by Mark is forgotten. It is, in fact, Isolde who first rejects Tristan's secret (unplanned) offer of help on the way to the ordeal—he is disguised as a beggar and clasps her knees asking for alms—and then, having taken the ambiguous oath, rejects him again when he approaches her. She does not wish her sanctity to be defiled. Immermann introduces the naked-sword motif at this point, as Isolde holds Tristan's sword between herself and him, so that he will not kiss her. It is she who banishes him, telling him that he may send for her only in his hour of death.

It is true that this development is only sketched out and might well have been changed or given a different slant, but it seems evident that the passionate and overwhelming love of the first part—"Free before the sun, the light and the sea, free before God who sees all"[39]—has later given way to a sentimentally moral attitude. Isolde takes the ambiguous oath,[40] but then renounces Tristan, in order not to tempt the Providence she has just cheated. Previously she had been prepared to forsake life rather than relinquish love, and to accept Brangane's sacrifice—of which Immermann makes much—in order to enjoy this love. Such a development as outlined is artificial and unconvincing.

The work also fails from other points of view, notably through the introduction of lengthy extraneous episodes which are Immermann's own invention. Immermann claimed: "What is conventionally chivalric or romantic . . . would disturb me and not come to life under my hands,"[41] and accordingly he supplied numerous minor characters and incidents which, while they are admirably suited to his humorous vein, are so lengthy and independent of the main story as to be distracting.[42] Any continuity of the main theme is entirely lost.

We have discussed Immermann's work at some length, since it is not only the first extensive modern adaptation but also an important source of material for poets through the nineteenth and into the twentieth century. We shall not discuss this particular aspect of the later versions, but it must at least be mentioned that Wagner himself must have derived some of his ideas from Immermann,—for example the idea of the suicide pact and the dramatic interruption of the shipboard love scene by the sighting of land.

Despite the interest of the Romantics in the literature of the Middle Ages and the Renaissance, despite the efforts of poets and scholars to revive and popularize the romance of Tristan and Isolde, the first half of the nineteenth century saw neither a successful poetic re-creation nor an adequate scholarly interpretation of the poem. Although published in various forms and with commentaries and explanations, the story achieved no great measure of popularity and remained, at best, a subject for learned polemics. The only version of Gottfried's work which dates from this period and which has attained some degree of acceptance is the translation made by Hermann Kurtz, which must be mentioned, if only in passing, since it served as the basis for Wagner's great music drama.

Kurtz's translation appeared in 1844 and was well received.[43] The second edition in 1847 also contained an introduction. There were later printings in 1877 and 1925, and although the work was superseded in some degree by that of Hertz (1877) and Pannier (1903),[44] it is still frequently quoted. The more important aspect of Kurtz's translation is, however, the introduction to the 1847 edition in which he discusses at some length the origins of the Tristan legend. This essay may contain what to us seem wildly inaccurate theories; but such theories were current at the time[45] and coincided sufficiently with Wagner's own views as to be a considerable stimulus in the latter's decision to use this material for an opera. Briefly, Kurtz sees the origin of both the Tristan and the Siegfried legend in the Osiris myth, which spread through Europe from East to West.

The idea of an opera on the subject of *Tristan and Isolde* first came to Wagner in 1854 when he was working on the *Ring*, and significantly enough the first reference to it occurs in a letter to Franz Liszt in which he tells of his discovery of the philosophy of Schopenhauer.[46] Although Wagner claims to find his own innermost convictions expressed in Schopenhauer's work —*The World as Will and Idea*[47]—there can be no doubt but that Schopenhauer's ideas had a considerable impact upon him, if only because he found them expressed in such a succinct and forthright manner. On the other hand it must also not be overlooked that Wagner was both influenced by Schopenhauer and incited to write his *Tristan* for purely personal reasons.[48] His relationship with Mathilde Wesendonck had reached a crisis which made life seem intolerable, and his experience of the torment of repressed passion led him to seek the sublimation of this experience in his creative work. This is probably the more genuine reason behind his decision to abandon temporarily work on the *Ring* cycle and to concentrate on writing an opera of normal proportions in order to relieve his pecuniary straits.[49]

In turning from the *Ring* to *Tristan* Wagner did not have to

move to a greatly different sphere for, like Kurtz, he believed in
the essential oneness of all mythical heroes. For him Siegfried
and Tristan were examples of what might be termed mythological
parthenogenesis, two aspects of the same figure and the same
problem: "Two seemingly unlike relations had sprung from the
one original mythic factor."[50] The astonishing thing is that he
was able to turn from the expansive treatment of the Siegfried
saga to a treatment of *Tristan* in which the action begins with the
crisis and the entire prehistory is either omitted or worked into
the dialogue.[51]

The plot of Gottfried's *Tristan*[52] has been reduced by Wagner
to the following situations: Act I the shipboard scene with the
drinking of the potion and the confession of love; Act II the
tryst and betrayal and wounding of Tristan; Act III the death
scene. Interwoven into the action of Act I is the story of the
earlier meeting of Tristan with Isolde and it is evident that she
loves him. From Tristan's behavior it is equally evident that he
loves her and cannot face her owing to his knowledge of having betrayed love by acting as an envoy for Mark. Rather
than face a loveless life at the side of Mark, Isolde determines to die and offers death also to Tristan by declaring
that before their arrival they must pledge each other as a symbol
of reconciliation for the death of Morold. Tristan knows that he
is being offered death rather than the dishonor of betraying
love and consequently accepts. They are both, therefore, determined to die and are deceived by Brangane who substitutes the
love potion for the poison. This substitution is not only important
for Wagner's theme, it also avoids the difficulty which has faced
all writers: how to make the potion credible to a modern audience.
Having drunk what they assume to be a death potion, Tristan
and Isolde are free to confess their love at the moment of expected death. The love potion is therefore not the origin of
their love which has long existed in repression, but the means
whereby it is brought into the open.

In the second act there is again a considerable amount of
recapitulation, this time not of earlier events but of the spiritual
development that has taken place after the abrupt intervention
of reality, as King Mark makes his appearance at the end of the
first act. Tristan has been slower to awaken to the truth than
Isolde since he was more deeply involved in worldly affairs,

but now both have become "*nachtsichtig*," that is to say, they are no longer blinded by the light of day, by worldly illusions; they await the coming of night. The realm of night is also the realm of love and of death, the time when the infinite becomes perceptible and the desire to be reunited with it grows stronger. Tristan and Isolde are individuals, individuated expressions of the infinite and thus separated still from each other by physical reality (the body), or—as they put it—by that little word *and*.[53]

Their suicide pact had, however, been wrong since their desire had been to escape *out of this world*.[54] They have now discovered that the world is illusion, have renounced it and with it all desire. They have achieved in love the state of non-will which is the right path: "if he [death] had to close the one door to us, Love has now guided us to the right door which she has chosen for us."[55] Their desire is therefore non-desire, the complete renunciation of desire in order to become one again through death with the universal will, with the Nirvana which to Wagner is the realm of night and love, the home of perfect because unindividuated and incorporeal love. The achievement of this goal, the triumphant entry of the lovers into the true sphere of the universal will, is the subject of the third act. In this act it is made clear that their suffering in life does not now derive from incompatibility with the world but from the knowledge that there is a greater sphere of being which they cannot yet enter. The passive love-death in complete self-denial is the true gateway to this sphere of eternal fulfillment.

Wagner's success with the Tristan material is due primarily to his reduction of the action to the absolute minimum in favor of a depiction of the spiritual development, and to his treatment of the potion motif. In Gottfried the potion symbolizes the compulsive nature of love and the lovers' release from the restrictions of conventional morality. In Wagner's work the potion frees the lovers in a different sense: having already expressed the desire to die, they feel, after drinking the potion, that they are no longer of this life. Their path leads henceforth out of this life into the darkness of the love-death and Nirvana. The spiritual development in Gottfried's epic is completely different, just as the very idea of suicide is impossible for him. His lovers achieve their *unio mystica* in the withdrawal into the love grotto, but the emphasis is on complete harmony of the physical and spiritual, on the withdrawal into the world of the spirit in this life. Wagner's lovers triumph over sensual passion to the extent of complete and utter renunciation of life in favor of death and entry into the voluptuous realm of universal love. In other words, Gottfried's lovers are (re-)united *at* death but not *in* death; Wagner's pagan concept of Nirvana, the realm of transcendent love, was not possible in Gottfried's day.

The purpose of this brief and generalized comparison is not to measure one achievement against the other, but to enable the differences to be seen more clearly. There can be no doubt but that Wagner's music drama is a work of genius in which the original theme has been preserved but reinterpreted in a strikingly original and modern manner. To a greater or lesser extent almost all later modern versions and sometimes even scholarly interpretations have been influenced by his work.

III *Literary Versions since Wagner*

In the latter half of the nineteenth century several attempts were made to dramatize the Tristan theme. Although it must be assumed that these were, in the main, inspired by Wagner's opera, the sources are varied. Some show evidence of direct borrowing from Wagner, but in others the influence of Immermann is also apparent, and certain motifs are derived from Gottfried, the chapbook, or other versions of the romance. In most cases the authors used, it seems, modern translations rather than medieval originals.

None of these dramas was in any way successful and, while our concern is not primarily with success or lack of success but with the degree of understanding of the basic theme, it is, nevertheless, clear that the failure of these works is, to a considerable extent, due to a lack of appreciation for the nature of the fable. The story of Tristan and Isolde is essentially a study in the development of a spiritual relationship; the other characters and the action being mere adjuncts. Wagner recognized this and cut the external action to the barest minimum, putting, of course, much of the emotional content into the music. The authors of the plays, faced by such problems as making the potion, Brangane's substitution or Isolde's attempted murder of Brangane credible, lacked the courage or skill to cut through these details; or they felt—and possibly rightly so—that a drama could not solely consist of inner development. Their efforts are, therefore, directed toward explanation, motivation, and supporting action, with the result that the relationship between Tristan and Isolde is overshadowed by episodes in which they are often only indirectly involved.

Some individual aspects of these attempts at "modernization" are not without merit,—such as Schneegans'[56] replacement of the potion by the song "There was a king in Thule," which Tristan and Isolde overhear and which draws them together; but on the whole they are ingenious rather than convincing. At times they are even less credible than the original, as for example the magic ring which replaces the potion in Weilen's work.[57] In order to demonstrate the nature of the changes which these writers wrought and the resultant attrition of the original theme, we shall refer in some detail to one specific work, the play by Friedrich Roeber. This is of greater interest since the original (very weak) version dates from 1838, that is to say from before Wagner's *Tristan*. Roeber returned to the subject sixty years later and rewrote it entirely.[58]

In Roeber's final version, Tristan arrives in Ireland after having killed Morold; but instead of killing a dragon he saves Isolde's uncle from assassination at the hands of rebels. In this way, he gains the opportunity to present Mark's embassy. The marriage offer is accepted and the potion error is made before they depart for Cornwall. The second Isolde is in Cornwall with her brother Kaedin, and she—who loves Tristan and thinks that her love is returned—is loved by Marjodo, who thus has an additional reason for his hatred of Tristan. There are the usual intrigues, in the course of which Tristan kills Kaedin, who attacks him for having insulted his sister. Isolde of Ireland continues to postpone her wedding with Mark, and when Mark banishes Tristan they arrange a meeting at which they are caught *in flagrante*. The two lovers are condemned to death, but Isolde Whitehand frees Tristan who, in turn, rescues Isolde and flees with her to the forest. Here they are found in a pitiable state by Mark—accompanied by Isolde—and Roeber employs the device he had used in his earlier version, namely that of having Tristan lay Morold's poisoned sword between them. Mark exchanges the swords but in the process wakens Tristan. In his panic, Mark wounds Tristan with the poisoned sword and carries off Isolde to Tintagel. The remainder of the work follows the usual plot, for Isolde Whitehand, who is vainly trying to cure Tristan and who is violently jealous of the first Isolde, kills him with the tale of the black sail. One important minor element which Roeber has retained from the earlier version, although in a less strongly developed manner, is King Mark's attachment to Brangane, who attracts him more than does Isolde and whom he clearly intends to marry after having forgiven the lovers.

It is obvious that the organization of this work is directed primarily toward avoiding such matters as the wedding-night deception and the adulterous relationship. The love theme is reduced to the simple level of love in conflict with duty, and nothing is done to suggest that there is anything out of the ordinary about their love or the situation. The problem is a purely social one, and the severity of even this problem is deliberately weakened by circumstances.

Precisely the same intent underlies the detailed motivation of the other dramas of this period. The aim is always to remove what is morally unacceptable—*"an gemeinem Erdenschmutz"* (Roeber, p. iv)—and to supply some kind of logical plot by reassembling various motifs from different sources. The resulting action is always more complex, and the interest is spread over a much larger cast of characters and subplots. The focus, therefore, shifts from the relationship between Tristan and Isolde to the conflict of their relationship with social conventions in the form of duty, honor, and so forth. Weilen may claim that "the highest principle on earth is love" (p. 122) and Schneegans that to follow the urges of one's heart is to follow "God's commandment" (pp. 173–74); but the tendency is always to portray the lovers as being forced to renounce their claims to love in life, and as being the victims of a tragic fate which prevents the consummation of their love. The guilt is borne by society and its laws, but the lovers themselves may not break these laws.

The only version of *Tristan* from this period to achieve any lasting recognition is not a genuine reworking of the story but a form of translation, namely the version by Wilhelm Hertz (1877).[59] Although this work has been highly praised for its literary merit and is still quoted as a translation—for example

by Weber who calls it "the 'classic' translation"[60]—it is, as Pannier
says, "hardly to be considered as a translation."[61] Hertz himself
leaves no doubt about his intent, for he states in his introduction
that his first task was "to abbreviate, that is, to omit trivial matters. . . ."[62] He omits not only whole episodes but shortens
others and simplifies many of the stylistically involved passages.
The net result is a reduction of the original work by a round
quarter of its original length and a considerable simplification
of the style. As a modernized and abbreviated version of Gottfried, Hertz's work is not without importance, but it is, for all
its readability, neither a modern adaptation nor a genuine translation.

The first full translation to be made of Gottfried's work in
the twentieth century was prepared by Karl Pannier for Reclam's
Universal Library. This and other such literal renderings of
Gottfried's work need not, however, concern us. Of much greater
interest is another modernization of the medieval Tristan legend,
which appeared in 1900, from the pen of the great French scholar
Joseph Bédier.[63] Bédier had long been studying the relationship
between the various medieval forms of *Tristan* and, in addition
to publishing the results of his work in learned journals, he
embodied the fruits of his research in a re-creation in modern
French of the "original" form of *Tristan,* basing himself upon
the extant fragments of Béroul, Thomas, and others. His "translation" is couched in such uniformly excellent style that the
work was enthusiastically received by critics—and awarded a
prize by the Académie Française—and was translated into German
by Julius Zeitler[64] and into English by Hilaire Belloc.[65] Together
with Louis Artus, Bédier later turned his prose work into a
drama, which was performed in Paris in 1929.[66] This was not
the first time that a scholar-poet had been inspired by the
Tristan theme; but the work of A. W. Schlegel in Germany or
of Matthew Arnold in England[67] never enjoyed the influence
which Bédier's version exerted. While he continued to make
contributions to Tristan scholarship, his literary version provided
the incentive and, in many cases, the material for later adaptations.

The number of versions of the Tristan story increases rapidly
after the turn of the century, and varied use is also made of the
theme, as for example by Thomas Mann in his *Tristan* novella,[68]

where the Tristan situation, the Wagner-Mathilde Wesendonck
relationship and the impact of Wagner's music are all combined;
or by James Joyce, who weaves the Tristan-Isolde relationship
into the complex fabric of his *Finnegans Wake*.[69] While dramatic
versions still predominate, versions in prose and verse are by
no means lacking. From this large and varied collection we can
do no more than select the most interesting and characteristic
examples. Since each work has, by now, so many predecessors
and, therefore, so many possible sources, the question of source
material will not be touched upon.

One of the earliest dramatic versions in the twentieth century
is Albert Geiger's *Tristan*.[70] In this work, Geiger reverts partly
to Gottfried by dividing his play into two parts, devoting the
first to Blancheflor and the second to Isolde. The two parts are
very closely linked by the figure of Tristan himself, by his resemblance to his father, and by a deliberate parallelism in action. In the first part, Geiger takes some liberties with his source,
for Blancheflor comes to Rivalin when he is wounded and is
persuaded by the force of his passion to give herself to him.
The ensuing night of love, in which Tristan is conceived, brings
about the death of Rivalin. Blancheflor confesses her fault and
is banished by her brother Mark; but she does not die until
after Tristan has grown up and she has seen in him the first
signs of his passionate nature, which he has inherited from his
father. Tristan's brief love affair with the shepherd girl occasions
the revelation of the true facts of his parentage.

The Isolde episode proper begins with the Tantris situation and
the violent reaction when it is discovered that he is the
slayer of Morold. In Geiger's version—where the incipient love
is very evident—Tristan is saved because he has rescued Isolde
from a bear while hunting. The wooing mission then follows;
but the potion is replaced by a poison—an overdose of sleeping
draught—which Isolde wishes to take but which is knocked from
her hand by Tristan. There follows the love confession which,
together with the love scene in Cornwall, is very Wagnerian.
The latter part of the story is, however, quite new and must
be Geiger's own invention. Tristan flees from Isolde, who aban-
dons Mark in search of him. Tristan comes to Parmenie, which
is ravaged by war and pestilence, and there he successfully intervenes in a battle but receives a severe wound. He is carried

off to an inn where he is recognized; and here he is found by Isolde, who has contracted the plague. After a brief reconciliation scene they die together.

The details and the organization of the plot are evidently directed, as in previous cases, at removing the incredible—there is no dragon, no potion, no grotto—while the Blancheflor episode has been expanded and emphasized in order to give foundation to Tristan's character. His passionate nature—*"dies allzu wilde Blut"* (p. 203)—he derives from his father, and his destiny is also foreshadowed in the relationship of his father and Blancheflor. But Tristan is conscious of his own nature, and the conflict is, therefore, to a large extent within himself. He "flees from himself, but yet cannot escape himself" (p. 202). His passionate attachment to Astrid, the shepherd girl, is easily overcome, and he also tries at first to resist the attraction of Isolde. As a result of the "potion scene," he gives way, but once banished from Cornwall, he is actually fleeing from Isolde who, as he knows, is searching for him; for "rather should God and Satan meet than I and she" (p. 209). At the end, he realizes the futility of trying to escape his destiny and of seeking to flee from himself. The passion which has driven the two lovers to wander restlessly through the world and has dragged them down from high position and luxury to the squalor of this inn has nevertheless been stronger than death. Now they meet in the presence of death and find peace: "So once, a long time ago, a woman came in love to my father, stepping over night and death with the light foot of longing. And gave him death and love. Death and love—in a bridal kiss—" (p. 219).

In contrast to Geiger, Emil Ludwig[71] adheres relatively closely to the medieval material—the chapbook form largely—but only through the use of lengthy and tedious passages, in which characters relate to each other, unconvincingly and at times tortuously, past events. The only interesting point lies in the explanation of the lovers' return from the grotto. When Mark finds them there, he exchanges swords, and they feel morally obliged to return to court, even though it is doubtful whether or not Tristan will be allowed to stay in Cornwall. There are also indications that their life—Tristan's life in particular—cannot be fulfilled in the absence of worldly activity. Only later Tristan feels unable to keep away from the court and disguises himself as a jester. The remainder of the action is abbreviated by his receiving a poisoned wound from Andret, whom he kills, when he reveals himself to Isolde.

The interest which has been noted in the subsidiary characters of the story (Brangane, Mark, and Isolde Whitehand), and which, at least in the dramatic versions, is primarily the result of the requirements of plot structure, now begins to increase. Emil Lucka, for example, wrote a prose work in which the central figure is Isolde Whitehand.[72] This work, apart from containing probably the worst prose[73] in any Tristan version known to us, also has the most fantastic plot. The effect of their passionate embrace on the vegetation in the garden of Tintagel is such that the whole garden blooms and remains in bloom until the wedding night of Tristan and Isolde Whitehand. At the moment of the erotically described consummation, the garden withers and Isolde of Ireland dies. Tristan returns to her—summoned by a swallow which taps at his window bearing a golden hair!—and together with her corpse he sails off into the mists of the sea. Between these two passages, there is a lengthy description of Tristan's relationship with Isolde Whitehand and her family, with all kinds of episodes culled from various sources.

The most interesting attempt, however, in the early twentieth century to study a specific aspect of the plot is undoubtedly Georg Kaiser's *King Cuckold*.[74] The character of King Mark differs from version to version and his age also varies. Frequently he is portrayed as being much older than Tristan, in order to win sympathy for Isolde—though not, it would seem, in Wagner—and Kaiser takes this even further by depicting Mark as extremely old and almost senile. All subsidiary characters, with the exception of the opponents of Tristan, are removed, and the entire action restricted to the relationship between the lovers and Mark after the marriage.

Tristan's detractors try to convince Mark that he is being deceived by Tristan and Isolde, but he does not want to be undeceived, although for rather different reasons than in Gottfried. Soon even Tristan's enemies realize that Mark does not want the truth to be exposed and depart in disgust. The truth would appear to be that Mark, unable to possess Isolde, divines the relationship between Tristan and Isolde and takes a vicarious pleasure in it. He is warming himself, as it were, with the heat of their passion. He is not anxious to disturb this situation and, therefore, does all he can to hinder Tristan's enemies and warn the lovers. He is tormented, however, by one question, by something which he has overheard and which threatens to destroy his peace. When Isolde welcomed Tristan in Ireland, she picked up her small six-year-old brother, stood him on her lap, and hugged and kissed him. The thought of this embrace, which is clear evidence of her desire to embrace Tristan, torments the King, who fears that the child may have felt sexual desire for Isolde. He feels himself, as it were, cheated of his (vicarious) possession of Isolde by this child, which had possessed her earlier, even incestuously. It is Isolde's refusal to answer his question about this event which drives him to banish them in a fit of jealousy, but as soon as he has done so, he realizes—despite the barons' claim that he will now find peace—that he has cut into his own flesh; for now they can enjoy their love and he can have no part in it.

The recall of the lovers from their banishment does not bring about any solution, for they are now aware of the King's knowledge of their relationship. Mark's encouragement of their love has the opposite of the desired effect. Their love, which had already withered, now dies completely, and Mark's pathetic attempt to persuade them to embrace only results in their feeling revulsion. The situation has thus become the complete reverse of the medieval one as portrayed by Malory; for now Mark kills them not because of their love, but because they are unable to love. In the final moments of the play, Mark once more clutches at a straw; this time it is the scarf which the dwarf has found and which, Mark claims, indicates that Tristan rather than he himself was the one deceived. In pathetic self-delusion he is, once more, "the happiest king in the world."[75]

Kaiser's work is important as the first attempt to make a thoroughly modern study out of the material, although he still retains the medieval situation. The King, who had in previous versions been seen either as a villain or, at best, as a misguided and un-understanding man who could not forgive until too late, is now seen in terms of modern psychology, and the problem is more his than theirs. This need not, however, be viewed as a break with tradition but rather as a natural development of the legend in keeping with the time.

Originally their discovery by the King had led the lovers to flee further into the forest; later they came back willingly to court. Already in the chapbook, their decision is motivated, to some extent, by the realization that the King knows about their affairs and that his generosity in not killing them in some way obligates them to him. From this point, it is but a short step to the treatment by Ludwig or Vesper;[76] and to the radical conclusion in Kaiser. Kaiser's apparently stringently modern interpretation is, in itself, a case study on the theme of the medieval precept: "Love seldom endures when it becomes known to others" (*"Amor raro consvevit durare vulgatus"*).[77]

The psychological complications of the triangle relationship are further exploited in Ernst Hardt's drama *Tantris the Fool*,[78] in which a single episode rather than a single figure has become the whole plot. The tenor of this popular episode was always humorous, even coarsely humorous: Tristan appeared as a fool at court and was able to make jokes about himself and Isolde, but at night he took off his fool's garb and came to Isolde. The love which, in Kaiser's version, is destroyed by the intervention of the King is shown in Hardt's drama to be defeated by circumstances: Isolde does *not* recognize Tristan in the fool and loses him.

At his banishment, Tristan together with King Mark and in the presence of witnesses, had signed a document to the effect that both their lives would be forfeit if he set foot in the land again. This document is the outcome of the plotting and deceit which had culminated in the ambiguous oath, which had never really convinced Mark. Since the day of Tristan's departure, the deception then practised publicly has been silently maintained; and an atmosphere of doubt and distrust pervades the action. The apparent reappearance of Tristan deceives Dinas, Tristan's friend, and through him also Isolde, but the revelation that Tristan has been seen in two different places at the same time makes this appearance equally ambiguous. The ambiguity is heightened by Denovalin's refusal—because of his love-hate relationship to Isolde—to say whether or not Tristan fled from him when called upon in her name. Isolde's avid desire to hear of Tristan arouses Mark, but he misunderstands her situation, for she now feels deceived by Tristan, since, by appearing but then running away, he has forfeited her love and, at the same time, caused her—under the terms of the contract—to forfeit her life. Mark is, therefore, enraged by her apparent sophistry. First showing a passionate interest in Tristan's presence, she then inveighs against his treachery in coming. In a blind fit of love-hate, Mark condemns her to be given to the lepers, at which point Isolde herself deliberately goads him by her repetition, in passionate terms, of the original ambiguous oath.

Disguised as one of the lepers, Tristan drives the others away and falls at Isolde's feet, but she, "knowing" that he has betrayed his love, spurns him. When Denovalin enters, Tristan kills him and leaps from the wall of the castle. Popular superstition immediately sees in this miraculous escape of Isolde and Denovalin's death evidence of the former's innocence and approval in the eyes of God. Reluctantly, Mark, for he is still unconvinced, takes her back. Despairing of ever knowing the truth, he cries: "And if anyone finds her in Tristan's bed, I'll kill him if he tells me" (p. 98).

Into the uneasy situation that follows, Tristan enters as jester. Despite his open admission of detailed knowledge of the relationship between Isolde and Tristan—he even calls himself Tantris—the truth is not believed but taken to be fiction or fool's license. Isolde, though deeply disturbed, is unable to recognize Tristan, and even when a stranger knight, brought in dying, admits that he was carrying Tristan's shield, which makes it evident that it was not Tristan who had fled, she is still unable to recognize him. In the last act, the fool pleads in vain for recognition. Then, when he hears that Husdant, Tristan's dog, is still alive, he joyfully goes to see it despite warnings that it attacks all those who approach. Isolde begins to have doubts, but it is too late. Tristan leaves the castle without a backward glance, the dog leaping joyfully along at his side. Unable to recognize Tristan in the fool, Isolde is left only with the hope of seeing him again in death.

The lovers and Mark are hopelessly involved in a situation that is largely of their own contriving but which they no longer control. Too deeply enmeshed in the web of deceit which they have woven, they are unable to free themselves from the deception of appearances. Only Mark, who suffers most, realizes his helplessness and admits in despair: "God is playing with me"

(p. 136). The result of this complex situation is to change love into hate; and the whole work seems to be largely concerned with the problem of the proximity of these two emotions. Such feelings underlie both Mark's and Denovalin's actions and even the lovers are confronted by the same problem, for in their inability to extricate themselves from the web of deceit they have cast around them as protection, misunderstanding and doubt cause their love to waver between love and hate and to prevent them from achieving mutual recognition. This is a genuinely tragic situation, and of all works on the Tristan theme in the modern period this play comes nearest to a meaningfully tragic interpretation, if only of a single episode.

The two works by Kaiser and Hardt represent the most convincing attempts to endow the medieval fable with modern significance. Other versions in the early part of this century, whether cast in dramatic, prose, or verse form, consist, for the most part, only of a superficial reorganization of the material, a juggling of heterogeneous elements into what seems to the author to be a logical and somehow meaningful order. In the main, the prose versions—with the exception of Lucka's work— depart less from the original than the dramas and at times even claim to represent the "original," as for example Arthur Schurig's work, which is entitled *The Story of Tristan and Isolde in the Original Breton Form.*[79] Actually, most of these prose re-creations cannot lay claim to scholarly or literary distinction.

In all these versions—even in Kaiser and Hardt—the medieval situation, that is to say, the *mise en scène,* is retained; and to some extent this may be considered as a major weakness, in that there is a discrepancy between the appearance of the figures on the stage and the meaning which their actions are supposed to have. Only in the last few decades has there been any strong reaction against the "historical" approach to myth and legend, a reversion to the medieval attitude, when the material was treated in purely contemporary terms. Apart from modernizing parodies of the Tristan theme—separately or in the general Arthurian context—which draw some of their humor from the juxtaposition of medieval and modern features,[80] there have been only a few attempts at transferring the theme systematically into the modern world, one of the most striking examples being

Jean Cocteau's film *L'éternel retour* which was made in 1942 and has become one of the classics of the cinema.

In German literature, as early as 1926, an attempt was made to put the Tristan theme into contemporary dress in the play by C. A. Bernoulli entitled *Tristan's Marriage*.[81] Although this work, which takes place in business circles in the United States, contains numerous details borrowed from Gottfried's work and references to Wagner, the net result is so absurd that it is kinder to assume the work to be a deliberate parody. At all events, we shall pass it over and conclude our discussion with a brief analysis of a highly successful contemporary version of the Tristan theme in prose—H. E. Nossack's *At the Latest in November*.[82]

In Nossack's novel the entire story has been reduced to the following events: Marianne (Isolde) has made a *mariage de convenance* with Max (Mark), an industrialist. She meets Berthold (Tristan) at a reception (potion scene) in his honor, following his acceptance of a literary prize. She feels immediately drawn to him and takes him home with her. After a brief scene with Max—returning from a business trip—they leave together. Following a period of happiness (love grotto) they become estranged and Marianne returns to her husband. When Berthold's new play is given its first performance in the city, he again comes to the house where she is waiting for him. They leave together but are killed when their car skids on a bridge.[83]

Neither Berthold nor Marianne has any contact with the world, for both have rejected its meaningless materialism. Berthold, as a poet, openly rejects it; while Marianne, although surrounded by possessions and engaged in social activity, remains entirely untouched by these aspects of her existence. Neither has any doubt about the significance of their meeting or of the necessity of breaking with the past. And yet their relationship does not seem successful, since they become estranged and Marianne returns to her husband, if only temporarily. How is this to be understood?

The hallmark of the protagonists of Nossack's works is their awareness of the futility of the material world and the proximity of another form of existence—or nonexistence.[84] The few who have this awareness are faced with the problem of living out their life in this world, while aware of another and more meaningful sphere, which they neither can nor wish to explain. They must, therefore, act out their part in the world—"I was just there by chance and went along with everything in order not to be noticed" (p. 41)—and wait patiently. The great danger for them lies in becoming involved with the world and thereby losing their precarious equilibrium: "One must continually be on guard. And sometimes it is only our own fault, because we think we can simply take part in things like other people" (p. 7).

When Berthold and Marianne meet, this balance is disturbed, for their previous life had been one based on withdrawal and dissociation. Now they are faced with the necessity of building a mutual relationship on this basis, and this they fail at first to do, since worldly desires, in particular possessiveness and *engagement*, lead them into the error of which Marianne had spoken in the very first lines: "We must not make any mistake, I wanted to say to him . . ." (p. 1). It is only after a period of separation and suffering that they reach the point of mutual understanding, and the logical result of the attainment of this state is their death to this world, the realization of Berthold's first words to Marianne: "*Mit Ihnen lohnt es sich zu sterben*" (p. 13).

Discussion of this complex novel could be carried much further and detailed parallels drawn with Gottfried's work, but enough has already been said to show its striking resemblance to certain basic aspects of the medieval romance. Above all it is the idea of the *electi*, the belief in a restricted number of people who have seen through and beyond the limited materialistic philosophy of the world, which seems to draw this work close to Gottfried. These are the noble hearts (*edele herzen*) who live in the world and conform outwardly to the worldly concept of honor (*êre*), but are willing to suffer and strive for something greater. They are willing to take the risk of a step out of the normal world;[85] and when a fuller experience is granted to them, it is a logical result that they should be lost to this world and find the other. What this other realm is, Nossack does not explicitly say, but he suggests a temporal co-existence, since Marianne tells the story from the standpoint of this other existence—that is, after death. In this too, we are reminded of Gottfried and his expression of the timelessness of myth: "Thus their life lives and their death lives. Thus they live still and yet are dead, and their death is the sustenance of the living" (238–40; p. 44).

IV   *Tristan Scholarship since Wagner*

Scholarly discussion of Gottfried's *Tristan* in German literary histories of the latter part of the nineteenth century does not depart from the pattern established by the earlier critics. It is even obvious that the compilers of these works are often more indebted to their predecessors than to their own close knowledge of Gottfried's work. Eichendorff,[86] for example, writing in 1857—when Wagner was working on his *Tristan*—repeats the old cliché that the relationship between Wolfram and Gottfried is similar to that between Klopstock and Wieland. He rejects Gottfried's work as plainly immoral but admits that it is beautiful in its own insidious way. There is nothing new in any of this, except perhaps the more colorful quality of Eichendorff's condemnation of Gottfried for having tried "to undermine and tear down the sublime edifice which Wolfram had raised up, in order to plant on the ruins amidst flourishing poisonous plants a comfortable and relaxing pleasure garden for the voluptuous enjoyment of emancipated human nature" (p. 76). The only novelty here lies in the suggestion that Gottfried's work does contain, concealed from the reader and unknown even to the author, a deeply moral import. Eichendorff does not explain this moral; perhaps he is referring to Docen's suggestion quoted above (p. 119).

The conviction that Gottfried lacked any "serious convictions" as König expresses it[87]—repeating a phrase used by Wackernagel in 1848—is not new, but it was carried to extreme lengths by Scherer in 1883.[88] This scholar represents perhaps the ultimate in uncritical condemnation, for he is capable not only of dismissing Gottfried's style as forced, precious, and distinctly inferior to Hartmann's, but also of claiming that the poet "followed [his source] almost slavishly," although "the actual poem he made use of is lost" (p. 158).

Convinced of the immorality of the work, Scherer finds some small consolation in the fact that the potion, while it "leads to deceit and immorality" is still "from a certain point of view . . . a moral power, for though an egoistic passion it yet goes contrary to egoism. . . . It makes him bad but never vulgar" (*ibid.*). In general, Scherer sees in Gottfried a bourgeois who enthusiastically and uncritically embraces the ideals of the nobility and defends them passionately in his work. This way of life allowed anything which did not "create a painful impression," that is to say, which did not offend against the rule of moderation in all things.

A similar though more moderately expressed attitude was shown by Friedrich Vogt (1901),[89] who sums up Gottfried's philosophy as follows: "Gottfried's ideal is a sanguine enjoyment of life. . . . The highpoint of life is love; not, however, the . . . calm happiness of marriage but free love which despises the [moral] law" (p. 205). Vogt has, however, a much clearer picture of Gottfried's relationship to his predecessors. He contrasts Eilhart's purely material interest with Gottfried's psychological portrayal and emphasizes that Gottfried compared with Thomas is subtler, more courtly, more humorous, and more refined. To some extent, he shares Scherer's views on the qualities of Gottfried's style, maintaining that he is too conscious a stylist, who spreads himself on the surface whilst Wolfram plumbs the depths. In his conclusion, however, Vogt is unable to deviate from the usual line, stating: "The poet's enthusiastic acceptance of the idea of the omnipotence of love must continually be invoked in order to help us to stomach the unpalatable material and the ethical indifference . . . which is only too evident" (p. 206).

At the same time as Vogt's work, there appeared a *History of Literature* by Bartels,[90] a work which is remarkable primarily for its direct opposition to Scherer. However, Bartels makes no contribution of his own to the interpretation of *Tristan*, restricting himself to such generalities as "Tristan's heroic nature is destroyed by passion, Isolde becomes completely bad, but they cannot part from each other" (p. 105)—a phrase strongly reminiscent of Scherer's definition of the original intention of the legend as being "to show how noble knighthood may be ruined by passion" (p. 159). Bartels also manages to introduce an element of chauvinism into his work by claiming that Gottfried's "concept of love is not low, it is . . . great and appropriate to our German conception, for we, far more than the Romance peoples, have always advanced the claims of passion" (p. 107).

Literary histories tend, at any period, to be conservative and directed toward a less well-informed public, so that one might be inclined to dismiss these examples as untypical were it not for the persistence and marked uniformity of attitude and for the lack of differing opinions in the scholarly journals. The more detailed works which appear in such journals are, at this period, concerned less with interpretation and more with questions relating to the sources and the interrelationship of the various versions and with the details of Gottfried's life. Neither the heated dispute over the origin of the Tristan legend nor the sometimes fantastic and totally unfounded theories about Gottfried's life need concern us here. Particularly in regard to the latter question we may accept Pfeiffer's statement: "Gottfried's life is completely obscure";[91] but the biographical approach cannot be entirely ignored since, as we have seen in connection with Scherer and others, it is not without influence on the critics' interpretations of the poem.

Excessive concern with biography is, in fact, one of the weaknesses of the only interpretative essay of any significance to appear in the late nineteenth century. In 1868 Richard Heinzel published an essay intended, as he put it, to be "a characterization not of his art . . . but of his person,"[92] and a large part of the essay is indeed given over to such questions as Gottfried's character and his station in life. Although Heinzel avoids the excesses of some earlier would-be biographers, he nevertheless deduces from *Tristan* that, among other things, Gottfried must have loved a lady socially his superior and that he was an ardent patriot. Fortunately, however, the general conclusions which Heinzel draws and on which he bases a brief but remarkably incisive interpretation of the poem are sufficiently vague as not to detract from the discussion. Gottfried was, Heinzel claims, bourgeois but well educated, and endowed with a great receptivity for love and beauty.

Although lacking in feeling for certain aspects of Gottfried's style and, above all, unable to appreciate the significance of the grotto allegory, which he dismisses as ruinous to the whole idea of life in the forest, Heinzel is the first to attempt an analysis of the love theme in its context and without reference to nineteenth-century mores. He states that everything else is inferior to the love relationship. Mark's attempt to come between the lovers is wrong and the subterfuge of the lovers is justified, including the so-called blasphemous oath which serves to illustrate the supreme value of love. This love has the power to resolve the conflict between the pursuit of personal happiness and the desire for the approval of others, between inclination and duty (*lîb* and *êre, Neigung* and *Pflicht*). Since this love is above the ordinary moral code and runs counter to the typical idea of minnesong, inclination or the demands of the body must be satisfied; but the outward form, that is, the demand for moderation (*mâze*), must also be met. This must be done in such a way as to achieve a harmony between desire and duty, to attain a harmonious union that will have honor (*êre*), by which is meant not general approbation but the tacit recognition and approval of the noble hearts (*edele herzen*), of the select few to whom it is given to understand and to strive for this kind of love.

This essay by Heinzel seems to have made no impression on other scholars in the last decades of the nineteenth century. The only other interpretative article of note from this period is one by Roetteken in 1890.[93] Roetteken stresses not only the futility of trying to judge Gottfried's work on the basis of a comparison with reconstructed theoretical originals, but also dismisses the biographical approach. His main concern is with certain aspects of Gottfried's technique and style; but in the course of his essay he shows some appreciation for the characterization of the protagonists. Regrettably, he does not go further in this direction of character analysis but falls back, instead, on the usual standpoint and concludes—apparently somewhat regretfully—that "Tristan is, for us at all events, an unattractive hero. All the greater is, therefore, our admiration for the poet's art which succeeds despite all in captivating us" (p. 114).

By 1900, then, surprisingly little progress had been made toward a genuine understanding of Gottfried's work. The main reason for this failure was the inability of the critics to free themselves from contemporary moral attitudes; and their confusion was compounded by the inevitable comparison with Wolfram. It is true that the two poets are poles apart and that they nursed an antipathy for each other, but to make the one the yardstick by which to measure the other is to ignore the existence of—or at least the necessity to look for—some objective criteria of judgment. Generally speaking, Gottfried's style was compared with Hartmann and judged as overly ornate; whereas his

subject matter was compared with Wolfram and judged ir-
religious. At most, the poet was excused by reference to the
French or Celtic, that is to say, inherently immoral nature of
the source material.

The early part of the twentieth century saw, at first, no great
advance in the understanding of the poem, although notable
progress was made in the study of the relationship of the various
medieval versions to one another and, in particular, of Gottfried
to his sources. In the main, the numerous histories of literature
remained conservative, while there were a few minor essays
which attempted to throw light on individual aspects of the
work. Of interest, for example, is an essay by an American
scholar, J. B. Shumway, who tries to overcome the traditional
view of Gottfried's work as an immoral tale clothed in beautiful form.[94] He discusses the morality of the poem, pointing to
the central importance of honor (*êre*) as it was understood by
Gottfried's audience and stressing also the different attitude
toward marriage in Gottfried's day. He concludes that the work
is a moral one, for it shows how two people are irresistibly
drawn to one another, how they resist but succumb, how they
are forced to all manner of subterfuge—involving great suffering
—and how they finally die a tragic death. While this view of
morality may not be accepted by modern critics, it is at least
an attempt to measure the poem against the standards of Gottfried's life and time—in particular the ethics of minnesong—and
show the conflict that underlies the story.

A second short discussion of Gottfried's work deserves mention at this point, although it was not published until 1933.
In 1907–8, Wilhelm Dilthey prepared lectures on the subject
of "Courtly Poetry and the National Epic," which contain a
brief study of *Tristan*.[95] Much of Dilthey's attention is directed
toward the usual comparison with Wolfram and the contrast
between Germanic and Romance elements. He calls *Tristan*
Gottfried's "gospel of joy, of beauty and of love, his freethinking
testament to passion"[96] but stresses also that the emancipated
spirit of the work in no way proves religious doubts on the part
of the poet; the religious basis of life remains untouched. Love
is for Dilthey a natural force (*Naturkraft*) which comes into
conflict with social convention. The symbol of this force is the
potion which brings about the indissoluble union of the lovers

and releases them from the bonds of convention: "The ethos of this high love is that all ideals are realized in the relationship of the lovers, that they then stand above all restrictions of society" (p. 140). The union of the lovers, Dilthey suggests, is like the mystic's union with God.

This mystical union of the lovers had been discussed before, but it was not until the publication of Friedrich Ranke's essay on the love grotto (1925) that the depth and import of this association was truly appreciated.[97] What had earlier been ignored or considered a major weakness of the poem,—namely the lengthy allegorical interpretation of the grotto,—is now seen by Ranke to be a fundamental aspect of Gottfried's doctrine. He points out that the allegory of the love grotto parallels the allegorical interpretations by the church fathers of the fabric, that is the actual structure, of the church. By deliberately relating his grotto, the worldly temple of love, to the Christian allegorical method of interpretation, Gottfried's concept of love becomes "a glorification of love raised to the level of religious fervor, a religion of love of astonishing boldness" (p. 12).

Although Ranke's discovery provides the starting point for modern interpretations of the poem and makes possible, for the first time, a real advance toward its understanding, it cannot be said that the resulting views show any great measure of agreement; on the contrary, they are at times quite contradictory. De Boor, for example, sees Tristan and Isolde as "love-saints" and the whole work as a kind of saint's legend.[98] At first only living on the lower level of worldly pleasure, they are raised, through the potion, to the higher world, of which the grotto is the temple. This is the world of love, but also of sorrow and suffering; it is a life of asceticism rather than of pleasure and clashes with the lower world of society. Mark is the representative of this lower world and thus the equivalent of the heathen, while Isolde Whitehand is cast in the role of temptress. The mystic union of the lovers is seen as being not only exemplary but even a spiritual sustenance—the bread of the prologue— to those who read it. While this religion of love inevitably involves its adepts in conflict with the lower world, the values of the latter are not portrayed as false; for these—marriage, for example—are the values of Christianity. Gottfried accepts this divine order of things and, according to de Boor, thereby skirts the problem of the relationship between this religion of love and the Christian *ordo*.

The association of the grotto with religious experience was taken much further by Julius Schwietering, who finds in *Tristan* extensive evidence of the influence of mystical writings, specifically those of Bernard of Clairvaux and his school.[99] For Schwietering the love of Tristan and Isolde is evident *before* the potion which merely awakens them to their love. The importance of this lies largely in the insistence on the absence of any reason for love; love cannot be earned, and preparedness is all. Equally there can be no guilt on the part of the lovers, for the love sphere is supreme: "The religious sphere is barely touched upon or, like the ethical, is subordinated to *minne*" (p. 190). According to Schwietering, "Gottfried has transformed the finite value of his ideal of love into an absolute, raised it to the level of the infinite and divine" (*ibid.*). In contrast to the religion of love, the forms and institutions of Christianity are reduced to mere form and formality. Although not prepared to make any assumption in regard to Gottfried's own religious beliefs, Schwietering points to an element of opposition to Christian concepts in his use of Christian motifs, for example the use of the idea of "eternal dying" for the acceptance of love in life in contradistinction to the Christian concept of death as the entry into the true life. Such a concept would naturally have made the conclusion of the poem problematical, and Schwietering does not attempt to theorize on this point but suggests that the problem, which Gottfried faced, of adapting to his own view the story of Isolde Whitehand, led him, in all probability, to abandon his work.

The most radically metaphysical interpretation of Gottfried's *Tristan* is to be found in Gottfried Weber's lengthy book entitled *Gottfried von Strassburg's "Tristan" and the Crisis in Medieval Thought Around 1200.*[100] Weber builds largely on the work of his predecessors but claims that *Tristan* is not analogous, but in direct opposition, to the Christian view of love. He stresses the fact that the lovers become one not in Christ but in each other and that the treatment of religious motifs and institutions is not merely disinterested but deeply skeptical. Beside the divine there is the daemonic, and it is to this latter sphere that the love experience belongs. The conflict between love and honor

(*minne* and *êre*) is an expression of the dualism with which
the church was at the time so deeply involved and leads to a
complete ambivalence of all values. Although Gottfried, according to Weber, has absorbed the influences of mysticism and
has made use of its modes and motifs, his work is primarily
symptomatic of the dualistic crisis in the thought of the early
thirteenth century, which found its most forceful expression in
the Cathar heresy, with which Gottfried has been linked by
Weber and others.

These religious-metaphysical interpretations have by no means
received general assent, and, in particular, the association of
Gottfried with Cathar or other heresies has been strongly denied.
There exists also a school of thought which sees rather the
courtly element as being predominant in *Tristan*. An example
of this view is found in the work of Friedrich Maurer.[101] He
rejects de Boor's thesis on every count and sees in the poem
primarily a conflict between love on the one hand and honor
and law (*êre* and *reht*) on the other. Honor and the law are
part of the natural order of things, aspects of the divine *ordo;*
but the conflict is not carried into the religious sphere. Law
and social restrictions are easily overcome by the power of love;
and it is basically the conflict with honor which brings about
suffering, separation, and eventual death. But it is the supreme
value of love to recognize the inevitability of this conflict and,
for its own sake, gladly to accept it and the sorrow and suffering
it brings. The suffering and death are, therefore, essentially un-
tragic, since they have been affirmed by the lovers in their acceptance of love.

Other interpretations of Tristan tend, in the main, to one or
another of these directions. Mergell, for example, stresses the
religious,[102] Bindschedler the courtly aspects.[103] Friedrich Heer[104]
is an exception insofar as he sees in Gottfried's work a radical
attack on the prevailing political order—"a frontal attack on the
courtly world" (p. 336). It is not our task here to criticize these
views individually or to compare them with each other. The
differences between them and our own view, as well as our
indebtedness to them, will be evident. The main question which
now arises is: Is there any consensus of opinion which might
indicate that we are now closer to a genuine understanding of

Gottfried's work than were the earlier critics, whose work we have rejected?

Scholars in the nineteenth century were to a large extent in agreement about Gottfried's work, but we have claimed that their agreement was based on a lack of understanding. They were favorably impressed by his style but were critical of the nature of the material and the lack of any moral or ethical standpoint on the part of the poet. Since Ranke's discovery we are closer to a proper understanding of *Tristan* insofar as the essential seriousness of purpose is concerned. The realization that in his poem Gottfried makes use of the forms and language of Christian allegorical exegesis and mysticism has led to a concentration on the metaphysical problem which it poses. It is generally accepted that the power of love is seen by Gottfried as being an absolute—something not earned or acquired as in minnesong and the Arthurian epics, but suddenly and irrevocably achieved. Gottfried propagates, in fact, a religion of love, and the basic question, therefore, concerns the relationship between this concept, its Christian counterpart, and its expression in the social order. So much seems agreed. Assuming, as we do, that the force of love cannot be judged in Gottfried's work to reside within the framework of the Christian religious experience, we are left with the possibility of love as a force analogous or equivalent to the Christian idea of love. The simple alternative seems to be either that love is a natural force contained within the divine order, with Satan being subordinate to the divine principle (the Christian view), or that it is an emanation of the principle opposing and co-existent with Christianity (the dualistic view). A conflict necessarily exists in either case, but its nature varies: in the former case the conflict can be resolved and is, therefore, in essence not tragic; in the latter the conflict is insoluble and tragic.

This outline of the two basic directions in Tristan scholarship is naturally a gross oversimplification, but it serves to throw into relief the significance of the theme of Tristan in the twentieth century and particularly for our time. We have said earlier that, while Gottfried's *Tristan* constitutes the best literary version of the material, the legend neither began nor ceased with him. It represents an elemental human problem in the form of a fable, a form that is at once viable and esthetically satisfying. The fable has consequently continued, through the centuries, to attract the attention of poets, scholars, and philosophers. Just as the literary versions of the theme have stressed now one and now another aspect, scholars too have read various meanings into Gottfried's work and in the theme in general. The problem which scholars have seen in Gottfried and the answers which they find there are as revealing of the scholars' own time as are the interpretations furnished by the poets. The general direction of scholarly research today is, therefore, indicative of the significance of the work in our own time, just as its reworking by Gottfried was for his.

V *Conclusion*

Passionate love, according to Denis de Rougemont, took its place in Western culture in the legend of Tristan and Isolde.[105] This dark passion is termed *eros;* and the ever smoldering crisis in European culture is seen as the conflict between *eros* and the Christian form of love, *agape.* The nature of *eros* is to consume itself with desire, to be in love with love itself rather than with the object of desire; for this object is finite, and *eros* is the yearning for the infinite. Whether this passion takes the form of the total renunciation of the presence of the beloved (*amor de lonh*), of complete sexual license, or of separation enforced by the social code, the final consummation can always be found only in death, when it passes beyond desire and reunites with the infinite. This basically dualistic belief irrupted in the late Middle Ages into violent conflict with the church, with the Christian concept of the all-embracing love of God as expressed, mythologically, in the incarnation and the crucifixion. Christian *agape* insisted, in particular, upon the marriage sacrament, the equal union of two individuals in this bond, and on neighborly love (*Nächstenliebe*) which should lead both persons to God.

Whether or not one agrees with de Rougemont regarding the historical origins and the nature of the distinction, it is clear that the conflict between what may simply be called passionate or romantic love and Christian love became an acute problem in the twelfth century. This theme of passionate love has remained a dominant aspect of European culture since that time, but the deeper problem was gradually reduced—as marriage became institutionalized—to a conflict between the sexual drive and social convention. It is for this reason that scholars and poets in the nineteenth century, living, as they did, in a strictly codified and "Christian" set of values, saw nothing in Gottfried beyond the problem of the conflict between sex and society. The only person to venture beyond this was the atheistically inclined Wagner.

In the twentieth century, these value systems have largely disintegrated. Instead, one is confronted on all sides by diametrically, and often violently, opposing forces which ignore moral codes and religious beliefs. But the relaxation of sexual taboos can, at most, relieve the superficial problem of the conflict between passion and society. The deeper existential problem remains and is, if anything, intensified by the very lack of established scales of values. The question still remains: How does the individual who rises above mere materialism and animal sensualism find fulfillment in love, and how can he reconcile this passion and experience with religion, that is, with the relationship between life and death? The Christian answer is a selfless love in Christ, which raises the lovers mutually to a spiritual fulfillment and a rebirth after life. The dualist's, atheist's, and pessimist's way is the abandonment of self to passion, the hope for extinction in possession, and the return to the infinite void. The middle way—Gottfried's way?—is to seek the refinement of the spirit in love in order to attain as much of heaven on earth as possible, to seek the spiritual union of souls in this world, and to leave the question of the life hereafter open.

Gottfried's work is unfinished, and without the conclusion no final statement on his philosophy can be made. Depending on the critic's own standpoint and his relation to his time, he will find one or the other answer in the work. But a final solution to the problem will never be found; perhaps it is, after all, symbolic that Gottfried's work remained unfinished.

Appendix

Gottfried's Environment

In Gottfried's day, Strasbourg was a relatively large and rapidly expanding center of trade in an area which was considered, agriculturally, one of the most prosperous.[1] The city had always been a bishop's seat and as such the center of extensive church domains; but until the beginning of the twelfth century the basic pattern of life had been purely agrarian. Strasbourg had been little more than a large village with a village pattern of existence. The unfree laborers and artisans had served the bishop's court, and the management of the affairs of the domains had been placed in the hands of the so-called ministerials.[2] By the middle of the twelfth century, however, this pattern had begun to change. With the weakening of the links between church and state, the bishop became less and less a representative of the state, and with the increase of population and superfluity of labor the system of soccage began to relax. Land was no longer only held in tenancy, and artisans began to work outside the limitations of their service to the bishop's court.

The increase in population and the rapidly developing trade along the Rhine attracted population from the surrounding countryside, although this was in no way indicative of a depressed state in agriculture. The result was an accelerated growth of the free population of the city. As it grew, it still came theoretically under the jurisdiction of the bishop and was still administered by his officers, but their interests came more and more to coincide with those of the population. Imperial policy was also interested in the growth of the new cities, not entirely for altruistic reasons, but also in order to gain centers of influence to counterbalance that of the church and the landowning nobility. Consequently, the relaxation of the soccage system and the change from payments in service or kind to payments in money were accompanied by the granting of Imperial city privileges in the form of releases from church taxation.

The administration of the expanding city was thus in the hands of the ministerials who had grown away from the church and who, though still nominally the bishop's representatives, formed the first rudimentary city council. This development had taken place by about the year 1200, at which time the city had probably acquired a population of about 10,000. The first city charter, granted in the early part of the twelfth century, had shown all the typical features of a purely church-controlled agrarian community. The second charter of 1214 shows a marked change in both form and emphasis, indicating an extensive and growing commercial life and a large degree of self-administration. The ministerials, as property-holding citizens, identified themselves with the new interests of the city and formed, together with the lower aristocracy and the merchants, a new and wealthy patrician class.

The cultural life of Strasbourg, in the absence of a secular court in which it might find expression, was equally in the hands of this new and ambitious patrician class, and a member of this class was presumably Gottfried's patron. But it must not be supposed that Gottfried wrote in any way exclusively for this class. Naturally his work must have been better appreciated by some than by others, but it was certainly read by the lay aristocracy, the knightly class, as much as by the patricians or the clergy. In fact we suspect that the poet derived some pleasure from the knowledge that his work would be read and enjoyed by those whom it, in fact, occasionally satirizes but who probably would not have been aware of the satire. At all events, the work was widely known and justly renowned. The number of manuscripts preserved is a legitimate guide to the status of any work, and in the case of *Tristan* we possess, whole or in part, over thirty manuscripts or approximately the same number as of *Das Nibelungenlied* and of Hartmann's *Iwein*.

Notes and References

Preface

1. Shortly after the completion of this study, the following abbreviated survey of the modern development of romantic love appeared in a popular magazine: "The 12th century—the era of romantic love, troubadours and chivalry. Courtly love at first may have been little more than a game. . . . Almost in spite of itself, however, something very important sprang from these artificial customs. Romantic love . . . raised as well the notion of consideration for a woman and loyalty to her. . . . It was not until the 16th century, however, that romantic marriage began to be a reality. . . . The English novelist Samuel Richardson, writing in the 18th century, is credited with being the first to say that love was needed for marriage. By the 19th century the idea was accepted generally." Ardis Whitman, "The Changing Ways of Love," *Redbook, The Magazine for Young Adults*, February, 1968, p. 120.

Chapter One

1. There is a considerable number of articles on the relationship between Wolfram and Gottfried. The most recent is F. Norman, "The Enmity of Wolfram and Gottfried," *German Life and Letters*, XV (1961/62), 53–67.

2. The edition of Gottfried's *Tristan* which has been used is that edited by Friedrich Ranke in 1930 and published in the ninth edition by Eduard Studer (Berlin, 1965). All quotations include, in addition to the line numbers of this edition, the page reference to the translation into English by A. T. Hatto (Penguin Classics, 1960), whose permission to quote we gratefully acknowledge.

3. Ed. Karl Lachmann, sixth ed. (Berlin, 1926); line numbers are in parentheses.

4. See *Deutsche Literatur des Mittelalters, Verfasserlexikon* (Berlin, 1933), Vol. I, Col. 620.

5. Ulrich's work is included in the Gottfried editions of E. von Groote (Berlin, 1821), F. H. von der Hagen (Breslau, 1823) and

H. F. Massmann (Leipzig, 1843). Quotations are taken from von der Hagen's edition.

6. Gustav Ehrismann, *Geschichte der deutschen Literatur bis zum Ausgang des Mittelalters* (Munich, 1949), vol. II, 2, i, p. 299.

7. Heinrich's works, ed. by Alois Bernt (Halle, 1906); his continuation of *Tristan* also edited by R. Bechstein (Leipzig, 1877).

8. Bodo Mergell, *Tristan und Isolde: Ursprung und Entwicklung der Tristansage des Mittelalters* (Mainz, 1949), pp. 188ff.; Magda Heimerle, *Gottfried und Thomas. Ein Vergleich* (Frankfurt, 1942), p. 164.

9. Friedrich Knorr, "Gottfried von Strassburg," *Zeitschrift für Deutschkunde*, L (1936), 10; J. Schwietering, *Die deutsche Dichtung des Mittelalters* (Darmstadt, 1957), p. 186.

10. M. J. Hartsen, *Der Zwiespalt in Gottfrieds "Tristan" und die Einheit der ritterlich-höfischen Kultur* (Amsterdam, 1938), p. 9.

11. Gottfried Weber, *Gottfrieds von Strassburg "Tristan" und die Krise des hochmittelalterlichen Weltbildes um 1200*, 2 vols. (Stuttgart, 1953), I, 306.

12. See below, p. 87ff.

13. Ed. V. Junk (Leipzig, 1928–29); line numbers are in parentheses.

14. *Herzmaere*, ed. E. Schröder, 3rd ed. (Berlin, 1959); *Trojanischer Krieg*, ed. A. von Keller and Karl Bartsch (Stuttgart, 1858–77; repr. Amsterdam, 1965); *Die goldene Schmiede*, ed. E. Schröder (Göttingen, 1926).

15. A comprehensive introduction to this manuscript by E. Jammers, *Das königliche Liederbuch des deutschen Minnesangs* (Heidelberg, 1965).

16. A very different interpretation is offered by Hermann Kurz, "Zum Leben Gottfrieds von Strassburg," *Germania*, XV (1870), 340ff.

17. See Ludwig Wolff, *Der Gottfried von Strassburg zugeschriebene Marienpreis und Lobgesang auf Christus* (Jena, 1924). The only recent attempt to vindicate this work for Gottfried is by Friedrich Heer, *Die Tragödie des heiligen Reiches* (Stuttgart, 1952).

18. On the acrostic see J. H. Scholte, "Gottfrieds von Strassburg Initialenspiel," *Beiträge*, LXV (1942), 280–302, and J. Fourquet, "Le cryptogramme du Tristan et la composition du poème," *Etudes germaniques*, XVIII (1963), 271–76.

19. A favorite acrostic is the Ave Maria; there are both Latin and German works in which the initial letters of lines or stanzas form the text of this prayer. See F. Tschirch, "Die Bedeutung der Rundzahl 100 für den Umfang mittelalterlicher Dichtungen: Studie zum symbolischen Denken im Mittelalter," *Gestalt und Glaube: Festschrift Söhngen* (Berlin, 1960), pp. 77–88.

20. For example by R. Bechstein in the *Allgemeine deutsche Biographie* (Leipzig, 1893), XXXVI, 502.

21. For the purpose of this study reference was made to the following manuscripts: M (Munich), H (Heidelberg), F (Florence), W (Vienna), B and O (Cologne), E (Modena), R (Brussels). We gratefully acknowledge the friendly cooperation of the authorities concerned.

22. Lines 28–29 (ed. H. Naumann and H. Steinger, Leipzig. Reclam, 1933), 4–5 (ed. H. Paul, Tübingen, 13th ed., 1966) and 3989 (ed. H. Paul, Tübingen, 13th ed., 1966), respectively.

23. This is a common feature of medieval poems. Compare, for example, the description of the upbringing of Alexander in the poem by the Pfaffe Lamprecht, ed. F. Maurer (Leipzig, 1940).

24. There are numerous theories about Gottfried's occupation. At one time he was thought, on the basis of a misreading of a manuscript, to have been city clerk (*rodelarius*) in Strassburg. For a summary of these theories see G. Weber, *Gottfried von Strassburg*, 2nd ed. (Stuttgart, 1965), pp. 4–6.

25. For a brief discussion of the environment in which Gottfried lived in Strassburg, see the appendix on pp. 151.

Chapter Two

1. The modern author feels it even necessary to stress that no resemblance is intended between the characters of his story and "any persons living or dead."

2. See, for example, the judgments from literary histories quoted below pp. 140ff.

3. The stages of development as described by Friedrich Ranke, *Tristan und Isolde* (Munich: Bruckmann, 1925) have been widely accepted. For a summary of the various views see Gottfried Weber, *op. cit.*, pp. 26ff.

4. A very popular subject in the Middle Ages, the earliest version dating probably from the eleventh century; St. Brenainn himself lived from 484 to 577.

5. One of the best known stories is that of Deirdre and Naisi, dramatized by J. M. Synge as *Deirdre of the Sorrows*.

6. By Bodo Mergell, *op. cit.*, chapter 2.

7. Marie de France lived *ca.* 1140–90. *Lays of Marie de France and Other French Legends*, transl. with an introduction by Eugene Mason (London, 1911).

8. Eilhart von Oberge, *Tristrant* (*ca.* 1180). The fragments edited by Kurt Wagner (Bonn/Leipzig, 1924) and the later reworking by F. Lichtenstein (Strassburg, 1877).

9. A German translation was made by Joh. Knieschek in the *Zeitschrift für deutsches Altertum,* XXVIII (1884), 261–358.

10. The chapbook version was edited by F. Pfaff for the Literarischer Verein (Tübingen, 1881).

11. Ed. Ernest Muret, 4th ed. (Paris: Champion, 1947).

12. The fragments of Thomas were edited by Bartina H. Wind (Leiden, 1950). A translation of the latter part of Thomas (after Gottfried breaks off) is included in Hatto's rendering (Chapter 1, note 2).

13. Published with translation into German by E. Kölbing. 2 vols. (Heilbronn, 1878–82). Page references are in parentheses. A convenient summary of the dependent northern versions with manuscript references is given by Paul Schach, "Some Observations on *Tristrams Saga,*" *Saga–Book,* XV, parts 1–2 (1957–59).

14. Ed. G. P. McNeill (Edinburgh/London, 1886).

15. *Chapbook,* p. 92. See above, note 10.

16. F. Piquet, *L'originalité de Gottfried de Strasbourg dans son poème de Tristan et Isolde* (Lille, 1905); A. Dijksterhuis, *Thomas und Gottfried: Ihre konstruktiven Sprachformen* (Groningen, 1935); M. Heimerle, *Gottfried und Thomas: Ein Vergleich* (Frankfurt, 1942).

17. This scene is discussed in detail below, p. 60.

Chapter Three

1. For a discussion of the major attempts at interpretation see pp. 145ff.

2. This is actually a slight simplification. Gottfried says: "Whatever demands he made on her, she met them to his satisfaction with brass *and* with gold" and refers explicitly to "false coin *of such nobility*" (12,601–3, 12,612; p. 207). Brangane is, after all, not a commoner.

3. This episode caused much distress to nineteenth-century critics and even now is, on occasion, referred to as being a blasphemy. See also below, p. 101.

4. The word occurs in lines 16,806, 17,079, 17,202, and 17,223. It is defined by Matthias Lexer in the *Mittelhochdeutsches Handwörterbuch* (Leipzig, 1869–78) as cleft, fissure, dwelling in withdrawal, hermitage, monastery, and womb. Hatto translates it twice as retreat and twice as refuge.

5. For a comparison of the two passages see below, p. 102.

6. The episode of the construction of the Hall of Statues is also lacking in Thomas, but a summary based on Bédier's reconstruction (discussed below, p. 130) is included in Hatto's translation.

7. See below, pp. 79ff.

8. The title—often misquoted—of a very interesting essay by J. H. Fisher, "Tristan and Courtly Adultery," *Comparative Literature,* IX (1957), 150–64.

Chapter Four

1. Petrus Tax, *Wort, Sinnbild, Zahl im Tristanroman* (Berlin: Erich Schmidt, 1961), pp. 169–170.
2. Although there have been several analyses of individual episodes, no attempt has yet been made to study the detailed structural relationships within the poem as a whole.
3. For example by J. G. Roeland, "Bilaterale Symmetrie bei Gottfried von Strassburg," *Neophilologus,* XXVII (1942), 281–90.
4. See M. S. Batts, "Numbers and Number Symbolism in Medieval German Poetry," *Modern Language Quarterly,* XXIV (1963), 349.
5. To us, the line numbers 9–12–6 do not have any special significance.

Chapter Five

1. Perhaps the worst example of this is offered by Wolfgang Golther in his *Tristan und Isolde in den Dichtungen des Mittelalters und der neuen Zeit* (Leipzig, 1907), where he condemns out of hand every modern version that does not follow implicitly his idea of the legend and respect also the sacrosanctity of Wagner's version.
2. It is also impossible to consider English versions of the Tristan theme where some great English poets of the nineteenth century achieved notable success. Scott's interest in the Middle English *Sir Tristrem* and his continuation of it are well-known, as are also the treatments by Arnold, Tennyson, and Swinburne. Swinburne's work in particular is a moving and provocative study of man's concept of sin and his attitude toward the divine in relation to the love experience. Interest in the theme does not cease by any means with the end of the Victorian era but has produced, in more recent times, versions couched in dramatic and fictional form. Thomas Hardy, Arthur Symons, and John Masefield are just a few of the better known names that could be mentioned.
3. A convenient listing of these versions is found in Paul Schach, "Some Observations on *Tristrams Saga,*" *Saga-Book,* vol. XV, parts 1–2 (1957–59).
4. Ed. G. P. McNeill (Edinburgh, 1886); an earlier edition by E. Kölbing (Heilbronn, 1882).
5. In his edition of the poem (Edinburgh, 1804).
6. Numerous manuscripts from the second half of the thirteenth century and incunabulae are extant. See E. Vinaver, *Etudes sur le Tristan en prose* (Paris, 1925).

7. The French version was several times printed in the fifteenth and sixteenth centuries but has never been critically edited; see below note 10.

8. Ed. Sir John Rhys for Everyman's Library, 2 vols. (London, 1906).

9. See Vinaver, *Le roman de Tristan et Iseut dans l'oeuvre de Thomas Malory* (Paris, 1925), pp. 109ff.

10. Quoted from Vinaver, *Le roman* . . ., p. 133. The only text available is *Le roman de Tristan en prose*, Tome 1, ed. Renée L. Curtis (Munich, 1963), which takes the story as far as the preparations for the departure of Tristan and Isolde from Ireland.

11. Critical edition by F. Pfaff for the Litterarischer Verein in Stuttgart (Tübingen, 1881). For a discussion of the various printings see pp. 203ff. Page numbers are given in parentheses for quotations from his edition. A new edition—not available at the time of writing—was prepared by Alois Brandstetter (Tübingen, 1966).

12. The *Meisterlieder* are most conveniently assembled in Eli Sobel, *The Tristan Romance in the Meisterlieder of Hans Sachs*, University of California Publications in Modern Philology, vol. 40, no. 2 (Univ. of Cal. Press, 1963). The *Tragedia mit 23 Personen von der strengen lieb her Tristrant mit der schönen Königin Isalden* in Hans Sachs, *Werke* ed. Adalbert von Keller, XII (Hildesheim, 1964), 142–86.

13. *Das Buch der Liebe inhaltendt herrliche schöne Historien allerley alten und newen Exempel, darauss menninglich zu vernemmen, beyde was recht ehrliche, dargegen auch was vnordentliche bulerische Lieb sey* (Frankfort, 1587).

14. *Werke*, ed. Hermann Palm (Darmstadt, 1961), I, 113. The play was first published in 1663.

15. *Histoire du chevalier Tristan, fils du Roi Méliadus de Léonois* April, I (Paris, 1776), pp. 53–238. Tressan calls it "le monument qui caractérise le mieux l'ancien esprit de Chevalerie & de la galanterie Françoises" (p. 53).

16. *Samlung deutscher Gedichte aus dem XII., XIII. und XIV. Jahrhundert*, vol. II (Berlin, 1785).

17. E. von Groote, *Tristan von Meister Gotfrit von Straszburg* (Berlin, 1821).

18. J. G. Büsching and F. H. von der Hagen, *Buch der Liebe* (Berlin, 1809).

19. *Vorlesungen über schöne Litteratur und Kunst*, (1803–4), part 3: "Geschichte der romantischen Litteratur" (Heilbronn, 1884), p. 12.

20. "Das Rittertum ist deutschen Ursprungs," *ibid.*, p. 35.

21. *Gedichte* (Heidelberg, 1811). In a letter dated September, 1802 Tieck had pointed out to Schlegel the impossibility of combining these diverse materials.

22. Carl Philipp Conz's *Gedichte* (Ulm, 1824) contains a poem on the subject of Tristan's death, while Wilhelm Wackernagel's *Gedichte eines fahrenden Schülers* (Berlin, 1828) includes a group of poems on the Tristan theme. Neither work has any poetic merit.

23. August Graf von Platen, *Sämtliche Werke*, ed. M. Koch and E. Peket (Leipzig, 1909), X, 373–82. See also the fragments of an epic poem in VIII, 269–75.

24. *Op. cit.*, p. 46.

25. In the *Leipziger Literatur-Zeitung*, 1812, reprinted in Jakob Grimm, *Kleinere Schriften* VI (Hildesheim, 1965), 84–100.

26. "Meister Gottfried von Strassburg," *Museum für altdeutsche Litteratur und Kunst*, I (1809), 52–61, 214.

27. Karl Lachmann, *Auswahl aus den hochdeutschen Dichtern des dreizehnten Jahrhunderts* (Berlin, 1820). The introduction is reprinted in his *Kleinere Schriften zur deutschen Philologie*, I (Berlin, 1876). The quotation is taken from p. 159 of the latter book.

28. G. G. Gervinus, *Geschichte der deutschen Dichtung* (Leipzig, ⁵1875). It appeared originally as *Geschichte der poetischen National-literatur* (Leipzig, 1835).

29. Heinrich Laube, *Geschichte der deutschen Literatur* (Stuttgart, 1839).

30. A. F. C. Vilmar, *Vorlesungen über die Geschichte der deutschen National-Literatur* (Marburg, 1845), p. 177.

31. Wilhelm Wackernagel, *Geschichte der deutschen Litteratur* (Basel, 1851–53), p. 200.

32. In the winter issue, 1839, pp. 126–85.

33. See below, p. 129.

34. *Tristan und Isolde* (Düsseldorf, 1841).

35. "In Eins geschmiegt / Schwelgen die schönen, die Erwählten" (p. 359).

36. "Klar sahen sich die beiden Seelen" (p. 368).

37. "Drum lass die Seelen, Liebster, ganz / Uns tauchen in den nassen Glanz, / Verschwimmen in dem süssen Gleichniß! / Ach! Wären wir doch auch Ereigniß / Wie das da drunten!" (p. 378).

38. "Auf, Tristan, hüten wir vor Schmach / Die treuen Seelen, reinen Leiber! / Hinunter groß and stolz und hehr / Zu Göttern in dem heiligen Meer!" (p. 382).

39. "Frei da vor Sonne, Licht und Meer, / Frei da vor Gott, dem höchsten Seh'r" (p. 356).

40. Isolde is actually hidden from view by a dust storm, and one hears the cry: "Sie hat's bestanden" (p. 440).

41. In a letter to Tieck (March 29, 1840), quoted from Golther (note 1), p. 274.

42. For example Ritter John's sea sickness or Brangane's storytelling as an interpolation during the potion scene.

43. *Tristan und Isolde von Gottfried von Strassburg*, uebertragen und beschlossen von Hermann Kurtz (Stuttgart, 1844). The spelling Kurz is later more frequently used.

44. For a discussion of Hertz and Pannier see below, p. 129f.

45. See, for example, F. J. Mone's introduction to the edition by E. von Groote (note 17).

46. Letter of December 16, 1854, written from Zurich. *Briefwechsel zwischen Wagner und Liszt* (Leipzig, 1887), II, 45–47. An abbreviated translation in *Letters of Richard Wagner*, selected and edited by Wilhelm Altmann, translated from the German by M. M. Bozman (London/Toronto, 1927), I, 273–74.

47. *Die Welt als Wille und Vorstellung*, ed. Löhneysen (Darmstadt, 1961).

48. Compare in this connection the personal incentive felt by Immermann to write his *Tristan*. Immermann indicates this himself in the "Zueignung."

49. See, for example, his letter of July 10, 1856 to his publisher Breitkopf and Härtel (Altmann/Bozman, I, 305–6).

50. "So waren auch . . . aus diesem einen mythischen Verhältnisse zwei anscheinend verschiedenartige Verhältnisse enstanden." *Epilogischer Bericht* to the *Ring des Nibelungen, Gesammelte Schriften und Dichtungen* (Leipzig, ³1898), VI, 267.

51. Not without some obscurity as, for example, in Tristan's reference to his parents at the beginning of Act III ("Is this the meaning then").

52. *Tristan und Isolde* was first published in Leipzig in 1859 and first performed in Munich in 1865. The text of the opera is in vol. VII of the *Gesammelte Schriften* (note 50).

53. "Doch das Wörtlein: und, wär' es zerstört . . . so starben wir um ungetrennt . . . der Liebe nur zu leben" (pp. 147–48).

54. Compare in this connection Schopenhauer's remarks, *op. cit.*, p. 680.

55. "Mußte er uns das eine Thor . . . verschliessen, zu der rechten Thür, die uns Minne erkor, hat sie den Weg nun gewiesen" (p. 49, lacking in the score).

56. L. Schneegans, *Tristan* (Leipzig, 1865).

57. J. Weilen, *Tristan* (Breslau, 1860).

58. F. Roeber, *Tristan und Isolde* (Leipzig, 1898).

59. *Tristan und Isolde von Gottfried von Strassburg* (Stuttgart, 1877). We have used the edition of 1923.

60. G. Weber, *Gottfried von Strassburg* (Stuttgart, ²1965), p. 80.

61. *Tristan und Isolde* (Leipzig, 1903), p. 6.

62. "Die nächste Aufgabe war, zu kürzen, d.h. Nebensächliches . . . auszustreichen" (p. v).

63. *Le roman de Tristan et Iseut* renouvelé par Joseph Bédier (Paris, 1900). A de luxe edition appeared in the same year with illustrations by Robert Engels, followed by numerous later editions and printings.

64. Leipzig, 1901.

65. London, 1903.

66. *Tristan et Iseut*, published in *La petite Illustration*: *Revue hebdomadaire* no. 231 (June 15, 1929).

67. See Arnold's lectures "On the Study of Celtic literature" (1865–66) and his poem *Tristram and Iseult* (1852).

68. In *Sechs Novellen* (Berlin, 1903).

69. London, 1939.

70. Karlsruhe, 1906.

71. *Tristan und Isolde* (1908). We have used the text found in *Dramatische Dichtungen* (Berlin, 1932).

72. *Isolde Weisshand* (Berlin, n.d. [1909]).

73. Their meeting is described, for example, as follows: "Sie fliegen aufseufzend zueinander und umklammern sich in jähem Ansturm; ihre Leiber biegen sich wie starke Bäume, über die Gewitter jagt. Tristans Mund wächst mit Isoldens Lippen zu einem einzigen Lippenpaar, sein Atem sengt ihre Wangen, daß rotes Feuer daraus aufschlägt, ihre Gesichter sind ein Blutkelch um die zuckenden Lippen" (p. 6).

74. *König Hahnrei* (Potsdam, 1913).

75. The phrase: "Ich bin der glücklichste König der Welt" occurs in Mark's first and last speeches and runs through the play as a kind of leitmotif.

76. "The King wants peace I know. . . . Shall we seek peace? I am willing to go to Bretagne or Spain." Will Vesper, *Tristan und Isolde* (Ebenhausen near Munich, 1911), p. 84.

77. Andreas Capellanus, *De amore libri tres*, trans. John J. Perry (New York, 1941); German version by Hanns M. Elster (Dresden, 1924).

78. *Tantris der Narr* (Leipzig, 1920).

79. *Der Roman von Tristan und Isolde in der bretonischen Urgestalt* (Dresden, 1923).

80. Wolfgang Golther (see note 1) and his student Erhard Heimann ("*Tristan und Isolde in der neuzeitlichen Literatur*" [Diss. Rostock, 1930]) show little appreciation of attempted parodies. This element of parody is present also in T. H. White, *The Once and Future King* (London, 1958).

81. *Tristans Ehe* (Leipzig, 1927).

82. *Spätestens im November* (1955). We have used the edition of 1963.

83. Only three subsidiary characters appear. Of particular interest is the resemblance between Blanck (Max's personal secretary) and Melot in Gottfried's poem.

84. The most detailed discussion of the metaphysical problem in *Unmögliche Beweisaufnahme*, part 3 of *Spirale* (Frankfort, 1956).

85. Here "einen Schritt außerhalb getan" (p. 113). Compare *Nach dem letzten Aufstand* (Frankfort, 1961), pp. 126–27, where the question of "survival" is also touched upon.

86. Joseph Freiherr von Eichendorff, *Geschichte der poetischen Literatur Deutschlands, in Werke*, ed. G. Baumann, IV (Stuttgart, 1958).

87. "Aber der Ernst der Gesinnung ist ihm durchaus fremd." Robert Koenig, *Deutsche Litteraturgeschichte* I (Bielefeld, [1878] ²⁵1898), p. 128.

88. Wilhelm Scherer, *Geschichte der deutschen Litteratur* (Berlin, 1883). We have used the translation of the third edition by F. C. Conybeare (Oxford, 1886).

89. Friedrich Vogt, "Mittelhochdeutsche Literatur" in *Grundriß der germanischen Philologie*, ed. Hermann Paul, vol. II, part 1, pp. 161–362.

90. Adolf Bartels, *Geschichte der deutschen Literatur* (Leipzig, 1901). We have used the fifth edition published in Leipzig in 1909.

91. Franz Pfeiffer, "Über Gottfried von Strassburg," *Germania*, III (1858), 59–80 (p. 80) in reference to J. M. Watterich, *Gottfried von Strassburg. Ein Sänger der Gottesminne* (Leipzig, 1858).

92. "Über Gottfried von Strassburg," in R. H., *Kleine Schriften*, ed. H. M. Jellinek and C. von Kraus (Heidelberg, 1907).

93. H. Roetteken, "Das innere Leben bei Gottfried von Strassburg," *Zeitschrift für deutsches Altertum*, XXXIV (1890), 81–114.

94. J. B. Shumway, "The Moral Element in Gottfried's *Tristan und Isolde*," *Modern Philology*, I (1904), 423–36.

95. "Die ritterliche Dichtung und das nationale Epos," in *Von deutscher Dichtung und Musik* (Stuttgart/Göttingen, 1957).

96. "Sein Evangelium der Freude, der Schönheit und der Liebe, seine Freigeisterei der Leidenschaft" (p. 138).

97. *Die Allegorie der Minnegrotte in Gottfrieds "Tristan"* (Berlin, 1925).

98. "Die Grundauffassung von Gottfrieds *Tristan*," *Deutsche Vierteljahrsschrift*, XVIII (1940), 262–306, and *Geschichte der deutschen Literatur*, II (Munich, 1953). We have used the 4th edition of 1960.

99. *Die deutsche Dichtung des Mittelalters* (Potsdam, 1940). We have used the edition published in Darmstadt, 1957. See also "Der *Tristan* Gottfrieds von Strassburg und die bernhardinische Mystik,"

reprinted in *Mystik und höfische Dichtung im Hochmittelalter* (Tübingen, 1960).

100. *Gottfrieds von Strassburg "Tristan" und die Krise des hochmittelalterlichen Weltbildes um 1200* (Stuttgart, 1953).

101. Chiefly in *Leid: Studien zur Bedeutungs- und Problemgeschichte besonders in den großen Epen der staufischen Zeit* (Bern, 1951).

102. Bodo Mergell, *Tristan und Isolde: Ursprung und Entwicklung der Tristansage des Mittelalters* (Mainz, 1949).

103. Maria Bindschedler, "Der *Tristan* Gottfrieds von Strassburg," *Der Deutschunterricht*, VI (1954, Heft 5), 65–76 and "Gottfried von Strassburg und die höfische Ethik," *Beiträge zur Geschichte der deutschen Sprache und Literatur*, LXXVI (1955), 1–38.

104. Friedrich Heer, *Die Tragödie des heiligen Reiches* (Stuttgart, 1952).

105. Denis de Rougemont, *L'Amour et l'occident* (1939), tr. as *Passion and Society* by Montgomery Belgion in a revised edition (London, 1956) and discussed at length by M. C. D'Arcy, S. J., *The Mind and Heart of Love* (New York, 1947). See also Denis de Rougemont, *Love Declared: Essays on the Myths of Love*, trans. Richard Howard (Boston, 1963). The book originally appeared under the title *Comme toi-même* (Paris, 1961).

Appendix

1. There is no satisfactory work known to us on the history of medieval Strassburg. There are brief discussions in more comprehensive works; for some details see G. F. von Schmoller, *Strassburgs Blüte und die volkswirtschaftliche Revolution im XIII. Jahrhundert* (Strassburg, 1875).

2. "The *ministeriales* were originally unfree personal servants holding the higher positions (butler, chamberlain, steward, etc.) at the courts of ecclesiastical and secular princes. At first maintained in their lords' households, they were later granted fiefs, the tenure of which was by special virtue of their office. This raised their social position, which was further improved when they were entrusted with political, military, and administrative powers. The extension of public administration from the 11th century onward caused this class of 'civil servants' to grow steadily." Quoted from *Encyclopaedia Britannica* vol. 15 (Chicago, 1965), 525.

Selected Bibliography

I Primary Sources
A. Gottfried's *Tristan*:
   1 Editions
   2 Translations
B. Medieval and Modern Versions of *Tristan*
C. Other Primary Sources.
  II Secondary Sources

PRIMARY SOURCES

I, A, 1 Gottfried von Strassburg: Editions in chronological order.

MYLLER, CHRISTOPH HEINRICH. B e r l i n, 1785 (*Samlung deutscher Gedichte aus dem XII., XIII. und XIV. Jahrhundert*, vol. II).

GROOTE, EBERHARD VON. Berlin: Reimer, 1821.

HAGEN, FRIEDRICH HEINRICH VON DER. Breslau: Josef Max, 1823. Contains also the continuations by Ulrich von Türheim and Heinrich von Freiberg, *Sir Tristrem*, etc.

MASSMANN, HANS FERDINAND. Leipzig: Göschen, 1843 (Dichtungen des deutschen Mittelalters 2); with the continuation by Ulrich von Türheim.

BECHSTEIN, REINHOLD. Leipzig: Brockhaus, 1869/70 (Deutsche Classiker des Mittelalters 7/8); with the continuation by Heinrich von Freiberg.

GOLTHER, WOLFGANG. Berlin: Speman, 1888/89 (Deutsche National-Literatur, IV, 2).

MAROLD, KARL. Leipzig: Avenarius, 1906.

RANKE, FRIEDRICH. Berlin: Weidmann, 1930, 9th ed. 1965. [Selections] Bern: Francke, 1946 (Altdeutsche Übungstexte 3).

I, A, 2 Translations into German.

MARBACH, GOTTHOLD OSWALD. *Die Jahreszeiten* (Winter, 1839), pp. 126–85.

KURTZ, HERMANN. Stuttgart: Rieger, 1844. Edition used: Stuttgart: Becher, 1847.

HERTZ, WILHELM. Stuttgart: Kröner, 1877. Edition used: Stuttgart: Cotta, 1923.

PANNIER, KARL. Leipzig: Reclam, 1903 (Universal-Bibliothek, Nos. 4471–76).

KRAMER, GÜNTER. Berlin: Verlag der Nation, 1966.

WEBER, GOTTFRIED. Darmstadt: Wissenschaftliche Buchgesellschaft, 1967. (Text, prose paraphrase and notes).

Translations into English.

WESTON, JESSIE L. London: Nutt, 1899.

ZEYDEL, EDWIN HERMANN. Princeton University Press, 1948.

HATTO, ARTHUR THOMAS. Penguin Classics, 1960.

B Medieval and Modern Versions of *Tristan;* in Chronological Order of Composition.

MARIE DE FRANCE. *Lais,* ed. Alfred Ewert. Oxford: Blackwell, 1947; ed. Jeanne Lods. Paris: Champion, 1959; trans. Eugen Mason. London: Dent, 1911 (Everyman's Library, No. 557).

BÉROUL. *Le roman de Tristan,* ed. Ernest Muret, 4th ed. Paris: Champion, 1947.

EILHART VON OBERG, *Tristrant I: Die alten Bruchstücke,* ed. Kurt Wagner. Bonn/Leipzig: Schröder, 1924. *Eilhart von Oberge,* ed. Franz Lichtenstein. Strassburg: Trübner, 1877.

THOMAS. *Les fragments du roman de Tristan, poème du XIIe siècle par Thomas* ed. Bertina H. Wind. Leiden: Brill, 1950. A translation of the fragments of Thomas in Hatto's translation of Gottfried.

BROTHER ROBERT. *Die nordische und die englische Version der Tristansage,* I: *Tristrams saga ok Isondar,* II: *Sir Tristrem.* Heilbronn: Henninger, 1878–82.

ULRICH VON TÜRHEIM. See the

Gottfried editions of Groote, Hagen and Massmann.

HEINRICH VON FREIBERG. *Tristanfortsetzung,* ed. Reinhold Bechstein. Leipzig: Brockhaus, 1877.

———, ed. Alois Bernt. Halle: Niemeyer, 1906. A translation in abbreviated form of the *Tristan* continuation is to be found in the English version of Gottfried by Jessie L. Weston.

Sir Tristrem, ed. Walter Scott. Edinburgh: Constable, 1804; ed. Kölbing (see BROTHER ROBERT above); ed. George Powell McNeill. Edinburgh: Blackwood, 1886.

Le roman de Tristan en prose, ed. Renée L. Curtis. Tome 1. Munich: Max Hueber, 1963. An abbreviated modern French version in the *Bibliothèque universelle des romans,* April, I (Paris: Eustache, 1776), 53–238.

Czech Tristan: German translation by Johannes Knieschek "Der čechische *Tristram,*" *Zeitschrift für deutsches Altertum,* XXVIII (1884), 261–358.

Tristran und Isalde [Chapbook], ed. Gotthard Oswald Marbach. Leipzig: Wigand, 1839; *Tristrant und Isalde,* ed. Fridrich Pfaff. Tübingen, 1881; ed. Alois Brandstetter. Tübingen: Niemeyer, 1966.

Buch der Liebe (full title page see Chapter 5, note 13). Frankfort: S. C. Feyerabents,

1587; ed. Johann Gustav Büsching and Friedrich Heinrich von der Hagen. Berlin: Dümmler, 1809.

MALORY, THOMAS. *Le Morte d'Arthur* (Caxton, 1485), ed. Sir John Rhys. London: Dent, 1906 (Everyman's Library, No. 45).

SACHS, HANS. *Tragedia mit 23 Personen, von der strengen lieb herr Tristrant mit der schönen königin Isalden, und hat 7 actus* (1553) in *Werke*, XII, ed. Adalbert von Keller. Hildesheim: Olms, 1964 (repr. of 1870 edition).

———. *Meisterlieder* in Eli Sobel, *The Tristan Romance in the Meisterlieder of Hans Sachs*. University of California Publications in Modern Philology, vol. 40, no. 2. University of California Press, 1963.

SCHLEGEL, AUGUST WILHELM VON. *Gedichte*. Heidelberg: Mohr, 1811.

CONZ, KARL PHILIPP. *Gedichte*. Ulm: Stettin, 1824.

WACKERNAGEL, WILHELM. *Gedichte eines fahrenden Schülers*. Berlin: Laue, 1828.

PLATEN, AUGUST GRAF VON. *Sämtliche Werke*, ed. M. Koch and E. Peket. 10 vols. Leipzig: Hesse, 1909. The verse fragment in VIII and the dramatic fragment in X.

RÜCKERT, FRIEDRICH. *Jung-Tristan* in *Die Jahreszeiten* (Summer, 1839).

IMMERMANN, KARL LEBRECHT. *Tristan und Isolde. Gedicht in Romanzen*. Düsseldorf: Schaub, 1841.

ARNOLD, MATTHEW. *Tristram and Iseult* (1852). Edition used: London: Macmillan, 1903 (vol. 1).

WAGNER, RICHARD. *Tristan und Isolde*. Leipzig: Breitkopf und Härtel, 1859.

WEILEN, JOSEF. *Tristan, Romantische Tragödie in fünf Aufzügen*. Breslau: Josef Max, 1860.

SCHNEEGANS, LUDWIG. *Tristan. Trauerspiel in fünf Aufzügen mit einem Vorspiel*. Leipzig: Otto Wigand, 1865.

GEHRKE, ALBERT. *Isolde. Tragödie in drei Akten*. Berlin: Heimann, 1869.

TENNYSON, ALFRED, LORD. *Idylls of the King*, "The Last Tournament" (1872). Edition used: Eversley edition. London: Macmillan, 1908.

SWINBURNE, ALGERNON CHARLES. *Tristram of Lyonesse* (1882). Edition used: Bonchurch edition by Edmund Gosse and Thomas James Wise in 20 vols. (vol. 4). London: Heinemann, 1925–27.

BESSELL, A. *Tristan und Isolde, Trauerspiel in fünf Aufzügen*. Kiel: Lipsius und Tischer, 1895.

ROEBER, FRIEDRICH. *Tristan und Isolde, Eine Tragödie. In zwei, nach Inhalt und Form verschiedenen Bearbeitungen von 1838 und 1898*. Leipzig: Baedeker, 1899.

BÉDIER, JOSEPH. *Le roman de Tristan et Iseut*. Paris: Piazza, 1900; German translation by Julius Zeitler (Leipzig: Seemann, 1901), and by Rudolf Georg Binding (Frankfort: Fischer, 1962); English translation by Hilaire Belloc (London: George Allen, 1903) and by H. Belloc and P. Rosenfeld (Pantheon Books, 1945).

GEIGER, ALBERT. *Tristan, Ein Minnedrama in zwei Teilen.* Karlsruhe: Bielefeld, 1906.

LUDWIG, EMIL. *Tristan und Isolde, Dramatische Rhapsodie* (1908). Edition used: *Dramatische Dichtungen.* Berlin: Zsolnay, 1932.

LUCKA, EMIL. *Isolde Weisshand, Ein Roman aus alter Zeit mit zehn Bildern von Emil Pretorius.* Berlin: Fischer, 1909.

VESPER, WILL. *Tristan und Isolde, Ein Liebesroman.* Ebenhausen bei München: Langewiesche-Brandt, 1911.

KAISER, GEORG. *König Hahnrei, Tragödie.* Potsdam: Kiepenheuer, 1913.

SYMONS, ARTHUR. *Tristan and Iseult.* London: Heinemann, 1917.

HARDT, ERNST. *Tantris der Narr.* Leipzig: Insel, 1920.

HARDY, THOMAS. *The Famous Tragedy of the Queen of Cornwall* (1916–23). Edition used: *The Dynasts . . . and the Famous Tragedy of the Queen of Cornwall.* London: Macmillan, 1931.

STUCKEN, EDUARD. *Tristan und*

Ysolt. Berlin: Reiss, n.d. [1916].

SCHURIG, ARTHUR. *Der Roman von Tristan und Isolde in der bretonischen Urgestalt.* Dresden: Aretz, 1923.

BERNOULLI, CARL ALBRECHT. *Tristans Ehe, Ein amerikanisches Drama in fünf Aufzügen.* Leipzig: Reclam, 1927.

MASEFIELD, JOHN. *Tristan and Isolt.* London: Macmillan, 1927.

WHITE, TERENCE HANBURY. *The Once and Future King.* London: Collins, 1958.

NOSSACK, HANS ERICH. *Spätestens im November.* Berlin: Suhrkamp, 1955. Edition used: Munich: Deutscher Taschenbuchverlag, 1963.

C Other Primary Sources.

CAPELLANUS, ANDREAS. *De amore libri tres,* trans. John J. Perry. New York: Columbia University Press, 1941; German translation by Hanns M. Elster. Dresden: Aretz, 1924.

DANTE ALIGHIERI. *The Divine Comedy,* trans. Henry Wadsworth Longfellow, ed. Henry Morley. London: Routledge, 1886.

GRYPHIUS, ANDREAS. *Werke,* ed. Hermann Palm. Darmstadt: Wissenschaftliche Buchgesellschaft, 1961.

HARTMANN VON AUE. *Gregorius,* ed. Hermann Paul and L. Wolff. Tübingen: Niemeyer, 1966. *Der arme Heinrich,* ed. Hermann Paul and L. Wolff. Tübingen: Niemeyer, 1966. *Iwein,* ed. H. Steinger. Leipzig: Reclam, 1933 (Deutsche Literatur in Entwicklungsreihen).

JOYCE, JAMES. *Finnegans Wake.* London: Faber and Faber, 1939.

KONRAD VON WÜRZBURG. *Kleinere Dichtungen,* ed. E. Schröder. 3 vols. Berlin: Weidmann, 1924–26. *Die goldene Schmiede,* ed. E. Schröder. Göttingen: Vandenhoeck und Ruprecht, 1926.

LAMPRECHT DER PFAFFE. *Alexander,* ed. Friedrich Maurer. Leipzig: Reclam, 1940 (Deutsche Literatur in Entwicklungsreihen).

MANN, THOMAS. *Erzählungen.* Frankfort: S. Fischer, 1959.

RUDOLF VON EMS. *Alexander,* ed. Victor Junk. Leipzig: Hiersemann, 1928–29 (Bibliothek des literarischen Vereins, Stuttgart, Nos. 272, 274).

SCHOPENHAUER, ARTHUR. *Die Welt als Wille und Vorstellung,* ed. Wolfgang Freiherr von Löhneysen. Darmstadt: Wissenschaftliche Buchgesellschaft, 1961.

SYNGE, JOHN MILLINGTON. *Collected Plays.* Penguin Books, 1952.

TIECK, JOHANN LUDWIG. *Ludwig Tieck und die Brüder Schlegel; Briefe,* ed. Henry Lüdeke. Frankfurt: Diesterweg, 1922.

WAGNER, RICHARD. *Gesammelte Schriften und Dichtungen.* 10 vols. in 5. Leipzig: Fritzsch, 3rd ed. (1897–98).

RICHARD WAGNER'S PROSE WORKS, trans. William Ashton Ellis. 8 vols. London: Paul, Trench and Trübner, 1893–99.

BRIEFWECHSEL ZWISCHEN WAGNER UND LISZT. 2 vols. Leipzig: Breitkopf und Härtel, 1887.

RICHARD WAGNER AN MATHILDE WESENDONK, ed. Wolfgang Golther. Leipzig: Breitkopf und Härtel, 1922.

RICHARD WAGNER TO MATHILDE WESENDONK, trans. William Ashton Ellis. London: Grevel, 1905.

LETTERS OF RICHARD WAGNER, ed. Wilhelm Altmann, trans. M. M. Bozman. 2 vols. London: Dent, 1925.

WAGNER, RICHARD. *Tristan und Isolde. Handlung in 3 Aufzügen.* English trans. by H. and F. Corder. . . . London: Eulenberg, n.d.

WOLFRAM VON ESCHENBACH. *Werke,* ed. Karl Lachmann. Berlin: de Gruyter, 6th ed., 1926.

II SECONDARY SOURCES

In order not to overburden this bibliography unduly, only works cited in the text are included, together with books and articles directly concerned with Gottfried's *Tristan* and *published* since 1940. For the period prior to 1940 see Heinz Küpper, *Bibliographie zur Tristansage* (Jena: Diederichs, 1941) and the additions and corrections by J. Horrent in *Revue belge de Philologie et d'histoire*, XXIII (1944), 357–63. For further items on general topics see the bibliographies in the works concerned, e.g., on love see the references to C. S. Lewis *et al.* in de Rougemont or D'Arcy.

ALER, J. M. M. *et al. Huwelijks trouw en Echtbreuk in de roman van Tristan en Isolde*. Amsterdam: Meulenhof, 1958.

ALLGEMEINE DEUTSCHE BIOGRAPHIE. 56 vols. Leipzig: Duncker und Humblot, 1875–1912. Gottfried von Strassburg is treated in vol. 36.

AMORETTI, GIOVANNI VITTORIO. "Gottfried von Strassburg l'artista," in *Saggi critici* (Torino: Bottega d'Erasmo, 1962), pp. 196–225.

ARNOLD, MATTHEW. "On the Study of Celtic Literature," in *Lectures and Essays in Criticism*, ed. R. H. Super. Ann Arbor: University of Michigan Press, 1962.

ARTHURIAN LITERATURE IN THE MIDDLE AGES, ed. Roger Sherman Loomis. Oxford: Clarendon, 1959. A collection of major essays including some on the *Tristan* versions.

ASHER, J. A. "Hartmann and Gottfried, Master and Pupil?" *AUMLA*, XVI (1961), 134–44.

BARTELS, ADOLF. *Geschichte der deutschen Literatur*, vol. I. Leipzig: Avenarius, 1909.

BATTS, MICHAEL S. "The Idealised Landscape in Gottfried's *Tristan*," *Neophil.*, XLVI (1962), 226–33.

———. "Die Problematik der *Tristan*dichtung Gottfrieds von Strassburg," *Doitsu Bungaku*, XXX (1963), 1–21.

———. "Numbers and Number Symbolism in Medieval German Literature," *Modern Language Quarterly*, XXIV (1963), 342–49.

BECKMANN, JANN-PETER. "Die Tristanromane Eilharts von Oberge und Gottfrieds von Strassburg. Eine Gegenüberstellung." Diss., Stellenbosch, 1962.

DI BENEDETTI, L. *La leggenda di Tristano*. Paris: Laterza, 1942.

BINDSCHEDLER, MARIA. "Tristan und Isolde," in *Freundesgabe für Eduard Korrodi* (Zürich: Fretz und Wasmuth, 1945), pp. 181–89.

———. "Der heutige Stand der Forschung über Gottfried von Strassburg," *Der Deutschunterricht*, V (1953, Heft 2), 90–94.

———. "Der *Tristan* Gottfrieds von Strassburg," *Der Deutschunterricht*, VI (1954, Heft 5), 65–76.

———. "Gottfried von Strassburg und die höfische Ethik," *Beiträge*, LXXVI (1954),

1–37; also issued separately Halle, 1965.

DE BOOR, HELMUT. "Die Grundauffassung von Gottfrieds *Tristan*," *Deutsche Vierteljahrsschrift*, XVIII (1940), 262–306.

————. "Der strophische Prolog zum *Tristan* Gottfrieds von Strassburg," *Beiträge*, LXXXI (Tübingen, 1959), 47–60. The above articles reprinted in *Kleine Schriften*, vol. I. ed. R. Wisniewski and H. Kolb (Berlin: de Gruyter, 1964). See also de Boor's interpretation in vol. 2 of his *Geschichte der deutschen Literatur von den Anfängen bis zur Gegenwart* (Munich: Beck, 4th ed. 1960).

BRINKMANN, HENNIG. "Der Prolog im Mittelalter als literarische Erscheinung," *Wirkendes Wort*, XIV (1964), 1–21.

DE BUGGER, I. M. "Tristan y Isolda y la investigacion moderna," *Boletin de estudios germanicos*, III (1955), 175–90.

CLOSS, AUGUST. "Gottfried von Strassburg *Tristan and Isolt*," in *Medusa's Mirror* (London: Cresset, 1957), pp. 57–82; a reprint of the excellent introduction to his partial edition (Oxford: Blackwell, 1958).

COMBRIDGE, ROSEMARY NORAH. *Das Recht im Tristan Gottfrieds von Strassburg*. Berlin: Erich Schmidt, 2nd ed. 1964.

DALBY, DAVID. "Der mære wild-

enære," *Euphorion*, LV (1961), 77–84.

D'ARCY, MARTIN CYRIL. *The Mind and Heart of Love*. London: Faber and Faber, 2nd ed. 1954.

DELBOUILLE, MAURICE. "Le premier Roman de Tristan," *Cahiers de civilisation médiévale*, V (1962), 273–86, 419–35.

DIJKSTERHUIS, AALTJE. *Thomas und Gottfried: Ihre konstruktiven Sprachformen*. Groningen: Noordhoff, 1935.

DILTHEY, WILHELM. *Von deutscher Dichtung und Musik: Aus den Studien zur Geschichte des deutschen Geistes*. Stuttgart: Teubner, 2nd ed. 1957.

DOCEN, BERNARD JOSEPH. "Meister Gottfried von Strassburg," *Museum für altdeutsche Litteratur und Kunst*, I (1809), 52–61, 214.

DUFHUS, ELISABETH. "Tristandichtungen des 19. und 20. Jahrhunderts." Diss. Köln, 1925.

EHRISMANN, GUSTAV. *Geschichte der deutschen Literatur bis zum Ausgang des Mittelalters*. 4 vols. Munich: Beck, 1959.

EICHENDORFF, JOSEPH FREIHERR VON. *Geschichte der poetischen Literatur Deutschlands*, in *Werke und Schriften*, vol. IV, ed. G. Baumann. Stuttgart: Cotta, 1958.

EIS, G. "Der Aderlass in Gottfrieds *Tristan*," *Medizinische Monatsschrift*, II (1948), 162–64.

————. "Fragment aus Gottfrieds *Tristan*," *Indogermanische Forschungen*, LX (1950), 90–94.

FISHER, JOHN H. "Tristan and Courtly Adultery," *Comparative Literature*, IX (1957), 150–64.

FOURQUET, JEAN. "Le Prologue du *Tristan* de Gottfried," *Bulletin de la Faculté des Lettres de Strasbourg*, XXXI (1952/53), 251–59.

————. "Sur l'acrostiche du *Tristan*," *Ibid.*, XXXI (1952/53), 197–200.

————. "Le cryptogramme du *Tristan* et la composition du poème," *Etudes germaniques*, XVIII (1963), 271–76.

FROMM, HANS. "Gottfried von Strassburg—eine Schlüsselgestalt des Mittelalters," *Valvoja*, LXXII (1952), 114–21.

————. "Zum gegenwärtigen Stand der Gottfried-Forschung," *Deutsche Vierteljahrsschrift*, XXVIII (1954), 115–38.

————. "Tristans Schwertleite," *Ibid.*, XLI (1967), 333–50.

FÜRSTNER, H. "Der Beginn der Liebe bei Tristan und Isolde in Gottfrieds Epos," *Neophil.*, XLI (1957), 25–38.

GANZ, PETER. "Polemisiert Gottfried gegen Wolfram?" *Beiträge*, LXXXVIII (Tübingen, 1966), 68–85.

GEERDTS, H. J. "Die Tristan-Rezeption in der deutschen Literatur des 19. Jahrhunderts,"

Wissenschaftliche Zeitschrift der Universität Jena, V (1955/56), 741–46.

GERVINUS, GEORG GOTTFRIED. *Geschichte der deutschen Dichtung*. Leipzig: Engelmann, 5th ed. 1871–74.

GNAEDINGER, LOUISE. *Musik und Minne im "Tristan" Gotfrids von Strassburg*. Düsseldorf: Schwann, 1967.

GOERKE, HANS. "Die Minnesphäre in Gottfrieds *Tristan* und die Häresie des Amalrich von Bena." Diss., Tübingen, 1952.

GOGALA DI LIESTHAL, OLGA. *Gottfried von Strassburg. Introduzione, traduzione e note*. Torino: Utet, 1955.

GOLTHER, WOLFGANG. *Tristan und Isolde in den Dichtungen des Mittelalters und der neuen Zeit*. Leipzig: Hirzel, 1907.

GREEN, DENIS HOWARD. "Konrads Trojanerkrieg und Gottfrieds *Tristan*: Vorstudien zum gotischen Stil in der Dichtung." Diss., Basel, 1949.

GRIMM, JAKOB. *Kleinere Schriften*. 8 vols. Hildesheim: Olms, 1965–1966.

GRUENTER, RAINER. "Der vremede hirz," *Zeitschrift für deutsches Altertum*, LXXXVI (1955/56), 231–37.

————. "Bauformen der Waldleben-Episode in Gottfrieds *Tristan und Isold*," in *Gestaltprobleme der Dichtung: Festschrift Günther Müller*

(Bonn: Bouvier, 1957), pp. 21–48.

———. "Das guldine lougen. Zu Gottfrieds *Tristan* vv. 17,536–56," *Euphorion*, LV (1961), 1–15.

———. "Das wunnecliche tal," *ibid.*, pp. 341–404.

———. "Der Favorit: Das Motiv der höfischen Intrige in Gottfrieds *Tristan und Isold*," *ibid.*, LVIII (1963/64), 113–28.

———. "*Daz ergest und daz beste*: Zu Gottfrieds *Tristan und Isold*, vv. 11,645–13,096," in *Medieval German Studies, Presented to Frederick Norman* (London: Institute of Germanic Studies, 1965), pp. 193–200.

Grundriss der germanischen Philologie, ed. Hermann Paul. Strassburg: Trübner, 2nd ed. 1900–1901.

HAHN, INGRID. *Raum und Landschaft in Gottfrieds Tristan*. Munich: Aidos, 1963.

———. "Daz lebende paradis, (*Tristan* 17,858–18,114)," *Zeitschrift für deutsches Altertum*, XCII (1963), 184–95.

———. "Zu Gottfrieds von Strassburg Literaturschau," *ibid.*, XCVI (1967), 218–36.

HALPERIN, MAURICE. *Le roman de Tristan et Iseut dans la littérature anglo-américaine au XIXe et au XXe siècles.* Paris, 1931.

HAMMERICH, LOUIS LEONOR. *Tris-*

tan og Isolde før Gottfried von Strassburg. Kopenhagen: Gad, 1960.

———. "Rationalismus und Irrationalismus im Tristanroman: Beobachtungen zur Vorgeschichte," *Mitteilungen des Universitätsbundes, Marburg* (1959), pp. 4–25.

HARTSEN, MARIA JACOTA. *Der Zwiespalt in Gottfrieds "Tristan" und die Einheit der ritterlich-höfischen Kultur.* Amsterdam: Swets und Zeitlinger, 1938.

HATTO, ARTHUR THOMAS. "Der minnen vederspil Isot," *Euphorion*, LI (1957), 302–7.

HEER, FRIEDRICH. *Die Tragödie des heiligen Reiches.* Stuttgart: Kohlhammer, 1952.

HEIMANN, EBERHARD. "Tristan und Isolde in der neuzeitlichen Literatur." Diss., Rostock, 1930.

HEIMERLE, MAGDA, *Gottfried und Thomas. Ein Vergleich.* Frankfurt: Diesterweg, 1942.

HEINZEL, RICHARD. "Über Gottfried von Strassburg," in *Kleine Schriften*, ed. M. H. Jellinek and C. von Kraus. Heidelberg: Winter, 1907.

HOLLANDT, GISELA. *Die Hauptgestalten in Gottfrieds "Tristan." Wesenszüge, Handlungsfunktion, Motive der List.* Berlin: Erich Schmidt, 1966.

JACKSON, W. T. H. "The Role of Brangaene in Gottfried's *Tristan*," *Germanic Review*, XXVIII (1953), 290–96.

————. "Tristan the Artist in Gottfried's Poem," *Publications of the Modern Language Association*, LXXVII (1962), 364–72.

————. "The Stylistic Use of Word-Pairs and Word-Repetitions in Gottfried's *Tristan*," *Euphorion*, LIX (1965), 229–51.

JAMMERS, EWALD. *Das königliche Liederbuch des deutschen Minnesangs: Eine Einführung in die sogenannte Manessische Handschrift*. Heidelberg: Lambert Schneider, 1965.

KANEKO, NAOICHI. Tristanstudien 3. Über den "muot" [jap.], *Jimbun Kangaku* III (1965/66), 121–53.

KASHIGAWI, MOTOKO. "Gottfrieds *Tristan*. Eine Analyse" [jap.], *Doitsu Bungaku*, XXIV (1960), 72–81.

KEMPER, RAIMUND. "Noch einmal wildenære," *Euphorion*, LVI (1963), 146–64.

KIRCHBERGER, LIDA. "Gottfried on Reinmar," *Monatshefte*, LVI (1963/64), 167–73.

KLEIN, K. K. "Das Freundschaftsgleichnis im Parzival-prolog. Ein Beitrag zur Klärung der Beziehungen zwischen Wolfram von Eschenbach und Gottfried von Strassburg," *Innsbrucker Beiträge*, 1/2 (1954), 75–94; reprinted in *Wolfram von Eschenbach* (below).

————. "Gottfried und Wolfram: Zum Bogengleichnis, *Parzival* 241,1–30," in *Festschrift für Dietrich Kralik* (Horn: Berger, 1954), 145–54.

KNORR, FRIEDRICH. "Gottfried von Strassburg," *Zeitschrift für Deutschkunde*, L (1936), 1–17.

KOENIG, ROBERT. *Deutsche Litteraturgeschichte*, vol. I. Bielefeld: Velhagen und Klasing, 25th ed. 1895.

KOLB, HERBERT. "*Der ware elicon*: Zu Gottfrieds *Tristan* vv. 4682–4907," *Deutsche Vierteljahrsschrift*, XLI (1967), 1–26.

————. "Der minnen hus: Zur Allegorie der Minnegrotte in Gottfrieds *Tristan*," *Euphorion*, LVI (1962), 229–47.

————. "Über den Epiker Bligger von Steinach. Zu Gottfrieds *Tristan* vv. 4691–4722," *Deutsche Vierteljahrsschrift*, XXXVI (1962), 507–20.

KURZ, HERMANN. "Zum Leben Gottfrieds von Strassburg," *Germania*, XV (1870), 207–36, 322–45.

LACHMANN, KARL. *Auswahl aus den hochdeutschen Dichtern des 13. Jahrhunderts*. Berlin: Reimer, 1820.

————. *Kleinere Schriften zur deutschen Philologie*. Berlin: Reimer, 1876.

LAUBE, HEINRICH. *Geschichte der deutschen Literatur*. Stuttgart: Hallberger, 1839.

MAURER, FRIEDRICH. *Leid. Studien zur Bedeutungs- und*

*Problemgeschichte, beson-
ders in den großen Epen der
staufischen Zeit.* Bern:
Francke, 2nd ed. 1961.

MEISSBURGER, GERHARD. *Tristan
und Isold mit den weissen
Händen. Die Auffassung der
Minne, der Liebe und der
Ehe bei Gottfried von Strassburg und Ulrich von Tür-
heim.* Basel: Reinhardt,
1954.

————. "Gottfrieds von Strassburg *Tristan* im Deutschunterricht," in *Germanistik
in Forschung und Lehre,* ed.
R. Henss and H. Moser (Berlin: Erich Schmidt, 1965),
pp. 20–31.

MERGELL, BODO. *Tristan und
Isolde. Ursprung und Ent-
wicklung der Tristansage des
Mittelalters.* Mainz: Kirch-
heim, 1949.

MITTENZWEI, JOHANNES. "Die
Überwindung der Welt des
Rittertums durch Musik in
Gottfrieds von Strassburg
Epos *Tristan und Isolde,*" in
*Das Musikalische in der Li-
teratur.* Halle, 1962.

MOHR, WOLFGANG. "Tristan und
Isolde als Künstlerroman,"
Euphorion, LIII (1959),
153–74.

MORET, ANDRE. "Le problème de
l'interpretation du Tristan de
Gottfried," in *Mélanges de
linguistique et de philologie,
Fernard Mossé in memoriam*
(Paris: Didier, 1959), pp.
322–29.

MOSSELMAN, FREDERIK. *Der Wort-
schatz Gottfrieds von Strassburg.* 's-Gravenhage: Excel-
sior, 1953.

NAUEN, HANS-GÜNTHER. "Die Bedeutung von Religion und
Theologie im *Tristan* Gottfrieds von Strassburg." Diss.,
Marburg, 1947.

NEUMANN, FRIEDRICH. "Warum
brach Gottfried den *Tristan*
ab?" in *Festgabe für Ulrich
Pretzel* (Berlin: Erich
Schmidt, 1963), pp. 205–15.

NORMAN, F. "The Enmity of
Wolfram and Gottfried,"
German Life and Letters, XV
(1961/62), 53–67.

OBER, PETER C. "Alchemy and
the *Tristan* of Gottfried von
Strassburg," *Monatshefte,*
LVII (1965), 321–35.

OCHS, E. "Gottfrieds wildenære,"
Archiv, CXCVII (1960),
126.

OKKEN, LAMBERTUS. "Gottfrieds
Tristan v. 10,383," *Zeitschrift
für deutsches Altertum,*
XCVI (1967), 237–38.

PANVINI, BRUNO. *La leggenda di
Tristano e Isotta.* Florence:
Olschki, 1951.

PENSA, MARIO. *Il Tristano di
Gottfried von Strassburg.* Bo-
logna: Pàtron, 1963.

PFEIFFER, FRANZ. "Über Gottfried
von Strassburg," *Germania,*
III (1858), 59–80; biographical; critique of Watten-
bach.

PFEIFFER, INGEBORG. "Untersuchungen zum *Tristan* Gottfrieds von Strassburg unter
besonderer Berücksichtigung

der altnordischen Prosaversion." Diss., Göttingen, 1954.

PIQUET, FELIX. L'originalité de Gottfried de Strasbourg dans son poème de Tristan et Isold. Lille: Université, 1905.

QUINT, JOSEF. "Ein Beitrag zur Textinterpretation von Gottfrieds Tristan und Wolframs Parzival," in Festschrift Helmut de Boor (Tübingen: Niemeyer, 1966), pp. 71–91.

RANKE, FRIEDRICH. Die Allegorie der Minnegrotte in Gottfrieds "Tristan." Berlin: Deutsche Verlagsgesellschaft für Politik und Geschichte, 1925.

————. "Zum Vortrag der Tristan-Verse," in Festschrift für Paul Kluckhohn und Hermann Schneider (Tübingen: Mohr, 1948), pp. 529–39.

RATHOFER, JOHANNES. "Der 'wunderbare Hirsch' der Minnegrotte," Zeitschrift für deutsches Altertum, XCV (1966), 27–42.

RICHTER, J. "Zur ritterlichen Frömmigkeit in der Stauferzeit. 1. Die Kreuzzugsidee in Wolframs Willehalm, 2. Der Mensch zwischen Gott und Welt in Gottfrieds Tristandichtung," Wolfram-Jahrbuch (1956), pp. 23–52.

RICKLEFS, JÜRGEN. "Der Tristanroman der niedersächsischen und mitteldeutschen Tristanteppiche," Niederdeutsches Jahrbuch, LXXXVI (1963), 33–48.

ROBSON, C. A. "The Techniques of Symmetrical Composition in Medieval Narrative Poetry," in Studies in Medieval French (Oxford: Clarendon, 1961), pp. 26–75.

ROELAND, J. G. "Bilaterale Symmetrie bei Gottfried von Strassburg," Zeitschrift für deutsches Altertum, XXXIV (1890), 81–114.

ROSENBERG, BRUCE A. "The Blood Mystique of Gottfried and Wolfram," Southern Folklore Quarterly, XXVII (1963), 214–22.

ROUGEMONT, DENIS DE. Passion and Society, trans. Montgomery Belgion. London: Faber and Faber, rev. ed., 1956.

————. Love Declared, Essays on the Myth of Love, trans. Richard Howard. Boston: Beacon Press, 1963.

SAVAGE, EDWARD B. The Rose and the Vine: A Study of the Evolution of the Tristan and Isolt Tale in Drama. Cairo: American University Press, 1961.

SAYCE, OLIVE, "Der Begriff 'edelez herze' im Tristan Gottfrieds von Strassburg," Deutsche Vierteljahrsschrift, XXXIII (1959), 389–413.

SCHACH, PAUL. "Some Observations on Tristrams-Saga," Saga-Book, XV (1957/59), parts 1–2.

SCHERER, WILHELM. A History of German Literature, trans. from the 3rd German ed. by F. C. Conybeare, ed. F. Max Müller. Oxford: Clarendon, 1886.

SCHIROKAUER, A. "Tristan 11,699," *Germanic Review,* XXII (1947), 90–91.

SCHLEGEL, AUGUST WILHELM VON. *Vorlesungen über schöne Litteratur und Kunst,* III, 1803–4. Heilbronn: Henninger, 1884 (Litteraturdenkmale des 18. und 19. Jahrhunderts, 19).

SCHMOLLER, G. F. VON. *Strassburgs Blüte und die volkswirtschaftliche Revolution im XIII. Jahrhundert.* Strassburg: Trübner, 1875.

SCHÖNE, A. "Zu Gottfrieds *Tristan*-Prolog," *Deutsche Vierteljahrsschrift,* XXIX (1955), 447–74.

SCHOEPPERLE-LOOMIS, GERTRUDE. *Tristan and Isolt. A Study of the Sources of the Romance.* Second ed. expanded by a bibliography and a critical essay on Tristan scholarship since 1912 by Roger Sherman Loomis. 2 vols. New York: Franklin, 1960.

SCHOLTE, J. H. "Gottfrieds von Strassburg Initialenspiel," *Beiträge,* LXV (1941), 280–303.

SCHRÖDER, FRANZ ROLF. "Die Tristansage und der persische Epos *Wîs und Râmîn*," *Germanisch-romanische Monatsschrift,* XLII (1961), 1–44.

SCHRÖDER, WALTHER JOHANNES. "Vindære wilder mære. Zum Literaturstreit zwischen Gottfried und Wolfram," *Beiträge,* LXXX (Tübingen, 1958), 269–87; reprinted in *Wolfram von Eschenbach* (below).

———. "Bemerkungen zur Sprache Gottfrieds von Strassburg," in *Volk, Sprache, Dichtung: Festgabe für Kurt Wagner* (Giessen: Schmitz, 1960), pp. 49–60.

———. "Der Liebestrank in Gottfrieds *Tristan und Isolt,*" *Euphorion,* LXI (1967), 22–35.

SCHRÖDER, WERNER. "Zur Chronologie der drei großen mittelhochdeutschen Epiker," *Deutsche Vierteljahrsschrift,* XXXI (1957), 264–302.

SCHÜLER, MEIER. "Sir Thomas Malorys 'Le Morte d'Arthur' und die englische Arthurdichtung des XIX. Jahrhunderts." Diss., Strassburg, 1900.

SCHULZE, URSULA. "Literarkritische Äußerungen im *Tristan* Gottfrieds von Strassburg," *Beiträge,* LXXXVIII (Tübingen, 1967), 285–310.

SCHUSTER, LUDWIG. "Neuere Tristandichtungen." Diss., Giessen, 1912.

SCHWARZ, W. *Gottfrieds von Strassburg Tristan und Isolde.* Groningen, 1955. (Antrittsvorlesung).

SCHWIETERING, JULIUS. *Die deutsche Dichtung des Mittelalters.* Darmstadt: Gentner, 1957.

———. "Gottfried's *Tristan,*" *Germanic Review,* XXIX (1954), 5–17.

————. *Mystik und höfische Dichtung im Hochmittelalter.* Tübingen: Niemeyer, 1960.

SHUMWAY, J. B. "The Moral Element in Gottfried's *Tristan und Isolde,*" *Modern Philology,* I (1904), 423–36.

SINGER, SAMUEL. "Thomas von Britannien und Gottfried von Strassburg," in *Festschrift für Eduard Tièche* (Bern, 1945), pp. 87–101.

SPARNAAY, H. "Der junge König Marke," in *Festgabe für L. L. Hammerich* (Kopenhagen: Naturmetodens Sproginst., 1962), pp. 281–89.

SPECKENBACH, KLAUS. *Studien zum Begriff "edelez herze" im Tristan Gottfrieds von Strassburg.* München: Aidos, 1965.

SPIEWOK, WOLFGANG. "Zum Begriff 'edelez herze' bei Gottfried von Strassburg," *Weimarer Beiträge,* IX (1962/63), 27–41.

————. "Zur Tristan-Rezeption in der mittelalterlichen deutschen Literatur," *Wissenschaftliche Zeitschrift der Universität Greifswald,* XII (1963), 147–55.

————. "Zur Interpretation des strophischen Prologs zum *Tristan* Gottfrieds von Strassburg," *ibid.,* XIII (1964), 115–18.

STACKMAN, KARL. "*Gîte und Gelücke.* Über die Spruchstrophen Gotfrids," in *Festgabe für Ulrich Pretzel* (Berlin: Erich Schmidt, 1963), pp. 191–204.

STEINHOFF, HANS HUGO. "Gottfried von Strassburg in marxistischer Sicht. Bemerkungen zu einer neuen Tristan-Interpretation," *Wirkendes Wort,* XVII (1967), 105–13; about Spiewok.

VAN STOCKUM, T. C. *Die Problematik des Gottesbegriffes im "Tristan" des Gottfried von Strassburg.* Amsterdam: N. V. Noord-Hollandsche Uitgevers, 1963.

STOLTE, HEINZ. *Eilhard und Gottfried: Studie über Motivreim und Aufbaustil.* Halle: Niemeyer, 1941.

TAX, PETRUS. *Wort, Sinnbild, Zahl im Tristanroman. Studien zum Denken und Werten Gottfrieds von Strassburg.* Berlin: Erich Schmidt, 1961.

TRIER, JOST. "Gottfried von Strassburg," *Die Welt als Geschichte,* VII (1941), 72–83.

TSCHIRCH, FRITZ. "Wernhers *Helmbreht* in der Nachfolge von Gottfrieds *Tristan,*" *Beiträge,* LXXX (1958), 292–314.

TUBACH, F. C. "The locus amoenus in the *Tristan* of Gottfried von Straszburg," *Neophil.,* XLIII (1959), 37–42.

————. "On the Recent Evaluations of the *Tristan* of Gottfried von Straszburg," *Modern Language Notes,* LXXIV (1959), 532–36.

VALK, MELVIN E. *Word-Index to Gottfrieds Tristan.* Madison: University of Wisconsin Press, 1958.

[*Verfasserlexikon*] *Die deutsche Literatur des Mittelalters: Verfasserlexikon,* ed. Wolfgang Stammler. 5 vols. Berlin: de Gruyter, 1933–55.

VILMAR, A. F. C. *Vorlesungen über die Geschichte der deutschen National-Literatur.* Marburg: Elwert, 2nd ed. 1847.

VINAVER, EUGENE. *Le roman de Tristan et Iseut dans l'oeuvre de Thomas Malory.* Paris: Champion, 1925.

———. *Etudes sur le Tristan en prose.* Paris: Champion, 1925.

VOGT, FRIEDRICH. *Mittelhochdeutsche Literatur,* see *Grundriss.* . . .

WACKERNAGEL, WILHELM. *Geschichte der deutschen Litteratur.* Basel: Schweighauser, 1851–53.

WAPNEWSKI, PETER. "Tristans Abschied: Ein Vergleich der Dichtung Gotfrits mit ihrer Vorlage Thomas," in *Festschrift für Jost Trier,* ed. William Foerste (Köln: Bohlau, 1964), pp. 335–63.

———. "Herzeloydes Klage und das Leid der Blancheflur: Zur Frage der agonalen Beziehungen zwischen den Kunstauffassungen Gottfrieds von Strassburg und Wolframs von Eschenbach," in *Festgabe für Ulrich Pretzel* (Berlin: Erich Schmidt, 1963), pp. 173–84.

WATTERICH, JOHANN MATTHIAS. *Gottfried von Strassburg, ein Sänger der Gottesminne.* Leipzig: Engelmann, 1858.

WEBER, GOTTFRIED. *Gottfrieds von Strassburg Tristan und die Krise des hochmittelalterlichen Weltbildes um 1200.* 2 vols. Stuttgart: Metzler, 1953.

WEBER, GOTTFRIED and HOFFMAN, WERNER. *Gottfried von Strassburg.* Stuttgart: Metzler, 2nd ed. 1965.

WEHRLI, MAX. "Der Tristan Gottfrieds von Strassburg," *Trivium,* IV (1946), 81–117.

WILLSON, H. B. "'Vicissitudes' in Gottfried's *Tristan,*" *Modern Language Review,* LII (1957), 203–13.

———. "Gottfried's *Tristan:* The Coherence of Prologue and Narrative," *Modern Language Review,* LIX (1964), 595–607.

———. "The Old and the New Law in Gottfried's *Tristan,*" *Modern Language Review,* LX (1965), 212–24.

WODTKE, FRIEDRICH WILHELM. "Die Allegorie des 'inneren Paradieses' bei Bernhard von Clairvaux, Honorius Augustodunensis, Gottfried von Strassburg und in der deutschen Mystik," in *Festschrift Joseph Quint,* ed. Hugo Moser (Bonn: Semmel, 1964), pp. 277–90.

WOLF, ALOIS. "Zur Frage des antiken Geistesgutes im *Tristan* Gottfrieds von Strassburg," *Innsbrucker Beiträge*, IV (1956), 45–53.

——. "Zu Gottfrieds literarischer Technik," in *Sprachkunst als Weggestaltung, Festschrift für Herbert Seidler* (Salzburg: Pustet, 1966), pp. 384–409.

——. "Die Klagen der Blanscheflur. Zur Fehde zwischen Wolfram von Eschenbach und Gottfried von Strassburg," *Zeitschrift für deutsche Philologie*, LXXXV (1966), 66–82.

WOLFF, LUDWIG. *Der Gottfried von Strassburg zugeschriebene Marienpreis und Lobgesang auf Christus. Untersuchungen und Text.* Jena: Bidermann, 1924.

Wolfram von Eschenbach, ed. Heinz Rupp. Darmstadt: Wissenschaftliche Buchgesellschaft, 1966.

Index